THE RESUME SOLUTION

By Da

This book is dedicated to my parents and family.

As with navigational bearings at sea, some relatives are relative; others are true. I have the great fortune to be attached to the latter.

Publisher & Contributing Editor: J. Michael Farr
Project Director/Interior Design: Spring Dawn Reader
Editors: JoAnn Amore and Charles Hammond
Production Editor: Lisa Farr
Cover Design: Mike Kreffel
Spot Illustrations: Mike Kreffel
Manuscript Preparation: Mary Croy

The Resume Solution—How To Write (and Use) A Resume That Gets Results
©1991, **JIST Works, Inc.**, Indianapolis, IN

Send all inquiries to:
JIST Works, Inc.
720 North Park Avenue • Indianapolis, IN 46202-3431
Phone: (317) 264-3720 • Fax: (317) 264-3709

Library of Congress Cataloging-in-Publication Data
Swanson, David, 1935-
    The Resume Solution / by David Swanson.
       p.   cm.
    "From JIST, The Job Search People"
    ISBN: 0-942784-44-8 : $10.95
    1. Resumes (Employment)   I. JIST Works, Inc.   II. Title.
HF5383.S92   1990   90-4904
650.14—dc20   CIP

ISBN: 0-942784-44-8

Foreword

Resumes are required. Even if you don't like them, they are required. There are times when you really should have one. They are important in the job-hunting and business scene.

But the scene has changed.

Resumes are no longer as important as they were, *say the people who receive them.*

Decades ago, the mail carrier brought mostly personal letters. Resumes were among the personal things received.

Now, the mail carrier usually brings catalogs ... third class mail ... flyers ... bulk pieces ... impersonal, often intrusive and unwelcome pieces of paper.

Today's resume is not as welcome. It comes with catalogs, with the "junk."

We must create these as very special examples of communication, pieces of paper which will get us in, not keep us out. Resumes are a combination of CALLING CARD, MESSENGER, and VISITOR. They are, indeed, very personal.

For twenty years, I have studied the various factors which make resumes GOOD and BAD.

I have personally read, and rated, more than twenty thousand resumes! (Most of these rated a 5 or below; a 10 is required!)

The Success Factors are relatively simple. But I have never seen all of them in book form before. And if they were written somewhere, the authors often minced words or gave you so many options that you never figured out which ideas were best.

You have in your hands a book which will put these secrets, this amazing system, within your reach ... and with very little effort.

You may react negatively to some of the things I tell you. That is your privilege.

But it is a resume reader's privilege to make judgments, to be the very best you can muster.

This book will do the trick for you.

Read.

Heed.

Succeed.

Table of Contents

Acknowledgements vi

Introduction: A Few Words On
Looking For A Job 1
   What This Book Is About 1
   The Odds Are Against Most Job Seekers .2
   So What's The Secret? 2
   My Style Is Your Style 3
   So How Do I Make My Resume
      Stand Out? 4
   Speed Reading Your Resume 4

Chapter 1: The Resume Basics . 5
   Start Your Job Search Right! 5
   A Few Words On Looking For a Job 6
   So What Are You To Do? 6
   Some Job Search Tips 6
   This Will Look Good On My Resume . . .8
   Resume Types .8
   Which Resume Type is Right For You? .13
   The Basics Of A Good Resume 16

Chapter 2: Collecting
Your Thoughts 17
   Collect, Organize, And Categorize 17
   The First Section, Identification 18
   Job Objective 21
   Education 23

Chapter 3: Tell 'Em What
Sells 'Em 29
   Why Are They Looking To Hire You—
      Or Anyone? 29
   What Are Accomplishments? 30
   What About Results? 31
   Analyze Your Work Experience 31
   The Basics: Selling Your Work
      Experience 32
   After You Have Documented Your Work
      Experience 35
   Personal Accomplishments 36
   Choose Your Most Impressive Results . 38
   Think Again 39
   What Others Say 39
   Special Skills 40
   Personal Information 40
   References 42

Chapter 4: Designing An
Outstanding Resume 49
   Tailor Your Resume For Excellence . . . 49
   The Eye-Strain Approach 50
   Edit, Edit, Edit 50
   How Long Should Your Resume Be? . . 51
   Secrets Of Readability 52
   How Do You Read, Learn, And Enjoy? 53
   Use Columns For Eye Appeal 54
   Be Your Own Art Director 56

Chapter 5: Packaging & Delivering Your Resume 59

Get Your Resume Noticed 59
Reproducing Your Resume 60
Make Your Resume First Class 62
Evaluating Your Print Shop 65
Selecting The Paper Stock For Your
   Resume 65
Final Touches 67
Stationery And Envelopes 67

Chapter 6: Sample Resumes & Worksheets 69

Choose A Style That Fits 69
30 Sample Resumes 71
Resume Worksheet 101

Chapter 7: The Cover Letter 109

The Cover Letter Is Your Introduction .109
Don't Send Cover Letters To Strangers 110
Tips On Writing A Good Cover Letter .111
Sample Cover Letters 113
Other Types Of Cover Letters . . .And
   Some Things To Avoid 116
Responding To Want Ads 117

Chapter 8: Saying Thank-You And Following Up 119

The Impact Of Good Manners
   And Thank-You Notes 119
Thanking People In Your Life 120
Send Thank-You Notes Or Cards 121
Some Tips On Writing Good
   Thank-You Notes 122
Some Sample Thank-You Notes 123
Follow-Up! 127
Keep Smiling 130

Chapter 9: Job Search Tips 131

Additional Tips For Your Job Search . 131
Private Employment Services 131
The State Employment Services 132
Personnel Offices 132
Applications 134
The Road Less Traveled: A More
   Effective Way 137
Networking—When It Works And
   When It Doesn't 138
Ask For An Interview Even If There
   Are No Openings 140
Keep Following Up 141
Use The Yellow Pages 142
Walk In, Anyway 143
Some Tips For Negotiating Salary ...143
How To Answer "the Big Question" . .146
What Comes Next? 147
A Final Word On Money 148

Epilogue: Is This The End? . 151

Adopt The Philosophy Of Job Hunting 151

Acknowledgements

Thanks to all of you:

To my family, for allowing me these thousands of hours to research and write.

To my friends, for their support.

To colleagues throughout the country and the world for their assistance.

To the people from my audiences who have written, called, and consistently encouraged and energized me.

Richard Nelson Bolles has been my mentor, teacher and a wonderful friend since we met in 1975, (and has written the book which all job-hunters should follow: *"What Color Is Your Parachute?"*) Although he and I share a distaste for the ways resumes are used and a sameness in philosophy about whether they should be used at all, he encouraged me in every way to write this book. I have been on Dick's workshop staff since 1977 and have treasured all of those moments, as well as his generosity, his counsel, and the support and affection of his wife and family.

Wayne Gartley, formerly Executive Director of the University and College Placement Association of Canada, is a superb writer; he brought knowledge, humor and a wonderfully light touch to the first drafts of this book when it was begun. Without his help and talents, there would be no book. And his television career is only now beginning.

Mike Farr and Debbie Featherston of JIST Works, Inc., not only run a good ship, and a tight ship, but a superb one. It is a joy to know a corporation whose heart is in The Right Place, which exists for the good of its employees and its clients. Thanks, Mike and Debbie, for your confidence and friendship. It is a privilege to be on your team.

And to the others, all of whom know how much they mean to me, because I tell them, probably too often: Scott, Ronald, Mike, Jayne, Ron, and many more ... someone is special.

Bueno...

Dave Swanson

Introduction

A Few Words On Looking For A Job

"Prepare the camel's hump in the usual way . . ."

So began a recipe I once saw in a gourmet cookbook.

Many job hunting books . . . and experts . . . and job counselors . . . offer the same sort of bewildering instructions: "Prepare your resume and take or mail it to employers."

It all sounds so easy!

Or does it?

What This Book Is About

This book is about writing a *superior* resume.

A resume that will stand out in a crowd. A resume that will be *read*.

This is also a book about getting a job. That is, I assume, your reason for wanting a resume to begin with.

The Odds Are *Against* Most Job Seekers

No matter how good your resume is (and most of them are *not* good at all), the odds are against most job hunters from the start.

Why?

Because they don't know how to write a good resume. Don't know how to use their resume. Don't know how the job market works.

Job hunters don't realize that employers may receive *hundreds*, or even *thousands*, of resumes every single week (whether the employers advertise for applicants in the newspaper or not) and that it is very easy for their resume to be lost in the shuffle.

This is especially true of large, well-known companies:

- Airlines
- Manufacturers of "brand name" products
- Broadcasting companies
- Advertising agencies

As an example, one airline, which hired some 300 flight attendants in one year, received over *750,000 thousand* letters, applications and resumes for these 300 positions. The astounding fact about all these resumes sent by job hunters every day is that the majority of them are incredibly poorly prepared.

They get only a fleeting glance from overworked, harried personnel directors before being tossed into the rejection pile.

What are the chances of the writer of a *poorly prepared* or *illegible resume being selected for an interview? Practically none!*

Scarce company resources make it impossible to interview every job applicant. (In most companies, it would take an army of interviewers working around the clock if all the people who applied for jobs were to be interviewed.)

And many (if not the majority of) resumes are from job applicants who are *not* qualified for the jobs for which they are applying.

These resumes get what they deserve to get—*rejected*. The people employed to screen resumes must weed out the unlikely job applicants; only the most promising people are selected for interviews.

The ratio of resumes to people selected may be 1,000-to-one or 100-to-one or 10-to-one in any particular company. But you can be sure that few of those who submit a resume will be called for a personal interview.

So What's The Secret?

There's no magic formula for getting a good job. Even the "perfect" resume can't do that for you. But I can help you increase your chances of getting that job by producing a superior resume.

And teaching you how to use it.

Like dieting, writing the best possible resume will take some hard work on your part. But the results will be well worth the effort.

I've read just about all the career planning/job hunting books that have flooded the bookstore racks in the past few years, but none of these has offered the inside information on the particular techniques of resume writing I will reveal in this book.

I do not intend to duplicate the excellent career planning/job hunting system explained by my mentor, Richard Nelson Bolles, in the best-selling *What Color Is Your Parachute?* Better you should buy a copy and read it immediately if you haven't already done so . . . and act upon the advice contained in this revolutionary book.

No, I am going to assume that you already have a pretty good idea of what skills you have and want to use in a job . . . and have pretty well defined some ideal job or jobs.

I'm going to show you how to develop a superior, readable resume. A resume that will produce the results you want.

And get you the job you want! The job that is right for you!

My Style Is Your Style

I'll give you tips that are guaranteed to make your resume superior-looking ... superior-reading . . . and will ensure that it gets *read*.

But the greatest gift I have for you is to enable you to do *your own resume*, using powerful secrets and proven techniques. To do otherwise ... to copy the standard "Harvard Graduate School of Business Resume Forms" ... or to turn over this chore to a "professional" resume-writing service ... would be a *mistake*.

Why? Because no one knows *you* like *you* do! And because if you go to one of the resume mills or career counseling outfits that also provides resume services, you maybe putting yourself in line for a slap.

Executives and personnel people aren't stupid. One "career counseling" firm (now thankfully forced out of business by a series of news articles and by the government itself) provided a "model" resume to each of its clients at "no extra charge."

So, for your $2500, they would package you into *their* recommended format. When personnel directors saw these resumes arrive (often several at a time), always printed on the same color paper and in the same slightly-unusual size, they knew what they had: people who weren't sharp enough to do a resume by themselves.

Those resumes, needless to say, found their way to the famed "circular file" via the fastest possible method. They weren't even paid the courtesy of a form-letter reply.

So, if you want it done right (and you want results from your resume)—do it yourself!

So, if you want it done right (and you want results from your resume)—do it yourself!

So How Do I Make My Resume Stand Out?

A resume is like an advertisement . . . a sales brochure of your special skills and training that will appeal to potential employers.

Of course, you are not qualified for every job that exists in today's complex employment market any more than one manufacturer's product is suited for every consumer's needs.

Nor would you want to work for every employer; nor in every job available. So you must do what any company with a product or service to sell does.

- Prepare your message so that it will be read and considered by your target audience—in this case, those who can hire you in a job of your choice.

- Evaluate your abilities accurately.

- Research your market fully.

Companies spend billions of dollars annually to produce advertisements that will appeal to readers of magazines and newspapers. They want you to *read* their message and *act upon it.*

Something in your resume must *click* . . . must grab the reader's attention, for it to be considered over all the others.

Speed Reading Your Resume

No one will spend much time reading your resume in detail. In fact, thirty seconds is a long time for the average screener to spend on a resume.

More likely, your resume will receive only 10 to 15 seconds of their time—unless you capture their attention immediately in the initial glance-through.

You must prepare your resume using the same techniques advertisers use, to give you an edge over your competition.

So that your resume will be *read!*

- Not ignored.
- Not passed over.
- Not rejected.

- But *read!*
- And *considered.*

You will learn how to design and test your resume for layout and readability. And to consider your resume's impact on potential employers.

And you will learn how to use a resume effectively in your job search. Which is what a resume is all about.

Or should be.

Chapter 1
The Resume Basics

Start Your Job Search Right!

Some frustrated people have used their resumes for wallpaper. But, more likely, you want to use yours for finding a *job*. Which seems reasonable enough. But you do need to realize a few facts:

- At its best, your resume may help you get an interview.

- If you use your resume in the traditional way—sending it to someone you don't know in a large organization—your resume is more likely to be ignored than read.

Before I begin to show you how to create a superior resume, it is essential that you understand how resumes are *best* used.

And why this is so.

A Few Words On Looking For A Job

Most job seekers believe they need to send out many resumes to personnel departments to get a job. And some do get jobs in just this way. But times are changing! About 75 percent of all business organizations don't even have personnel offices. They are small organizations, where over *seventy percent of all new jobs are being created.*

So if you insist on sending out resumes to personnel departments, you are missing most of the available jobs. And much of the opportunity.

Even organizations that *do* have personnel departments are far more likely to "file" your resume than do anything helpful with it. They get entirely too many resumes to do otherwise. So they will give yours a quick look over and then put it away, in all probability, with the others, there to rest for eternity. Or until someone throws it away.

In the unlikely event that your resume just happens to come in when an appropriate job opens up—for someone with just your experience and training—you might get an interview. But probably not, because it is more likely that your resume was set aside, in the reject pile. Rejected, even though you could do the job. Because your resume was dull. Or because it was too long. Or whatever the case.

The person who looked it over, along with the 25 (or 200) other resumes in the pile, had no idea of the dedicated person you are. They just had your resume. And it didn't catch their attention.

So What Are You To Do?

You, because you have read this book (and have done all the activities), will have a superior resume. Your resume will stand out from all the others. And get you the attention you deserve. But you should also understand that most hiring is not done by a stranger hiring an applicant who is unknown to her or him. Hiring is generally done by people who know an applicant already. So your next employer will probably be someone you know. And one of the reasons you'll be hired is because they will know you and *trust* you. They will also believe that you can do the job and that you will do it reliably and well.

No resume can do this whole "getting hired" process for you. Not even the one I will show you how to create. Only *you* can do the real work of getting hired.

Some Job Search Tips

I will give you more job search tips throughout this book, particularly in the last chapter.

But there are several important points for you to remember:

Someone You Know, And Who Likes You, Will Hire You

- You probably don't know them yet, nor do they know you. But you will meet during your search for a job. And you will like each other enough to work together.

- Which brings up an important fact that you should not ignore: most people get their jobs—as many as 40 percent of them—from leads provided by friends or relatives or acquaintances. Not from someone they don't know. So your task is to avoid, as much as possible, depending on strangers. Resumes sent to "Dear Mr./Ms. Personnel Department" will be treated just the way you treat the "Dear Occupant" mail you get. Like junk mail, they will be discarded, with few exceptions.

You Can Get To Know Almost Anyone

- I was once told that you can get to almost anyone, even the President, through just three to six levels of personal contact. Just ask someone you know for the name of someone *they* know who knows the President. And so it is in the job search. The process is called *networking*. For example, ask each of your friends and relatives for the name of someone who might know of a job opening that requires a person with your skills. You will come to know more people than you could ever imagine. If you ask this same question of each person you are referred to, you will meet more people than you can count. And one of them will hire you!

You *Can* Get To Know People Who Work In Large Organizations

- It's not difficult to get the name of the person in any organization who is most likely to hire someone like you. You can ask your friends and relatives if they know anyone who works there—or if they know someone else who might know. Or you can use the Yellow Pages to call the organization. And ask them, "Who is in charge of such and such?" In most cases, you can get right to them. Ask if you can come in to see them about any future job openings, even if none are open just now. *Then* send them your resume. And a thank you note for their precious time. Even if they can't see you now.

- It takes only a minute or so to make these personal contacts. And they can make *all* the difference.

Always Be Honest

- Your resume does not need to mention that you eat crackers in bed. We all have things we don't tell strangers. But it is dishonest to say you can handle something you cannot or that you have done something you have not done. Too many job seekers think they have to overstate what they can do to get hired. And as a result, too many resumes are not believable.

- Most employers will see right through an inflated resume. They won't hire a dishonest person. Nor would you. But some people do convince employers to hire them for jobs they can't do well. And, too often, they then lose the jobs. Or, even worse, they come to hate their jobs. And themselves. So, while this book is about creating delightfully *readable* resumes, it is also about getting a job. A job you can grow in. And enjoy.

"This Will Look Good On My Resume"

It's amazing how many people have used this reason for taking a certain job or training. We've all said it (and we've heard others say it) over and over again. It's as if we feel that everything we do in our work life must make our resume look good. But your resume should present a mirror image of your life (seen in the best possible light) rather than vice versa. And I'm now going to take you, step by step, through the construction of a superior-looking resume—a resume that will work wonders for you in your job hunt.

A Resume That Will Be *Read*.

Resume Types

Before you begin writing your resume, you need to be aware of the different types of resumes. There are at least seven different types of resumes:

- Chronological
- Functional (also called a skills resume)
- Narrative
- Combination
- Teaching
- Curriculum Vitae
- Creative

If all this seems confusing, remember: if it looks like a duck, walks like a duck, and quacks like a duck, it's a duck! A resume is a resume is a resume—no matter how you design it or what name you give it. The chief distinction between types of resumes is whether they are *chronological* or *functional*.

Chronological Resumes

A *chronological* resume stresses time—*when* you went to school or had a certain job. Thus you state in your resume that from September 1988 to May 1989 you worked at Foster Steel Foundries or you attended Bloom College. Every year, every month, every day of your working life is accounted for in such a resume.

Functional (or "Skills") Resumes

A *functional* resume stresses skills and is organized by skills, duties, or functions as shown in the example that follows later in this chapter.

Sample Chronological Resume

The resume on the following page illustrates a typical chronological resume which lists organizations where you have worked. They are listed in *reverse* order, beginning with your present, or most recent, employer. Your *first* full-time job is listed last and is usually given less space. You give less-detailed descriptions of accomplishments, duties, and responsibilities of your earliest jobs.

Chronological resumes are the most commonly used type. Because employers are used to seeing them, they find chronological resumes easy to read and follow.

Judith A. McGinty
7038 West Edgerton Street
Milwaukee, Wisconsin 53214
(414) 555-4465
(414) 444-4661 (messages)

CAREER OBJECTIVE:
Customer Service Supervisor/Manager

WORK EXPERIENCE:

1987 to 1990 **Guard Insurance Company**
Milwaukee, Wisconsin

Customer Service Administrator
Provided customer and general agent information in Pro Division. Processed policy changes, agent commissions, bill adjustments and corrections, audits, and accounts receivable in excess of $15 million. Utilized CRT system daily. Received "Service Management Award."

1986 to 1987 **Wrap n' Ship**
Milwaukee, Wisconsin

Store Manager
Authorized new account credit approvals, monitored collections, followed-up on slow-pays, provided information for customer billing and equipment. Sold additional telephone services.

1985-1986 **Telephone Information Systems**
Milwaukee, Wisconsin

Customer Service Representative
Managed retail store providing UPS,m wrapping, packaging, shipping and other services. Supervised three employees. Resolved customer problems. Maintained all permanent records for business.

1984 to 1986 **Real Estate Sales Agent**
Independently listed, presented and sold real estate properties.

EDUCATION

• Mount Mary College, Milwaukee
Completed 31 credits in business courses

• University of Wisconsin-Milwaukee
Completed additional courses for degree in
Public Relations and Mass Communications.

Sample Functional Resume

The typical functional resume lists the kinds of *functions* you performed on the jobs you have held. The functions are grouped together by their relationship to one another or by projects or assignments. This resume emphasizes the *skills* you have, rather than the places you have worked or the periods of time you worked at each organization. *Functional* resumes are used less often than *chronological* resumes.

You needn't always include dates in a *functional* resume, and you can account for your employment history in terms of the skills you used rather than the dates you worked. Lengths of time such as "Three Years" may be included. And names of companies may (or may not) be given depending on your preference.

There are pros and cons for each type.

Barbara H. Martinson
9612 W. Capstan Road
Sea View, California 92134
(714) 555-1537
Message: (714) 555-1657

JOB TARGET: Computer Programmer, using COBOL,
                               UNIX, C, or similar languages

SCHOOL ACHIEVEMENTS:

- **Honor Student**, Mount Diablo City College, Sea View, California. Graduate with Associate Degree in computer technology, May, 1990. 3.42 grade average.

- **Student Leader** in various campus organizations; President, Office Education Association; member, Student Council (2 years); chairperson, Campus Ride Pool.

- **High School Honor Student**. Active in various sports, clubs, musical organizations.

WORK EXPERIENCE

- **Organized and ran office** for local insurance office (four agents); Developed new filing system. Operated IBM PC with terminal access to IBM main frame. Developed and implemented new claims reminder procedures for agents. Improved own typing speed from 55 wpm to 75 wpm.

- **Raised $4,000 for charity** through Office Education Association fund drive, pizza sales; proceeds went to Special Olympics.

- **Selected as Laboratory Assistant** in Data Processing Lab at school. Used background knowledge to advise insurance agency on new hardware and software purchases for office.

PERSONAL

- Earned own school expenses. Worked at insurance office (above) and at supermarket while in high school. Hardworking, willing to relocate.

Which Resume Type Is Right For You?

If you have an excellent work record and educational background and you can account for each segment of your life, the chronological resume may be fine for you. But if you have any gaps that you don't want to include in your resume (like the year you were unemployed because you just didn't feel like working . . . or backpacked around Europe . . . or whatever), including dates will immediately raise the question, "What was she doing during this time?" Employers are suspicious of gaps in a resume. When they spot a gap, or a period of months or years you don't explain, they assume the worst. If your resume omits the months and years in which you worked at each place, you'll be "suspect."

Remember—the traditional selection process is a negative one. Employers use resumes to screen people out. They toss out many resumes before they choose the small number of people they will consider hiring. You might use a functional resume if the dates when you acquired your skills or worked in a particular job have little to do with the job you're applying for now.

Absolutely right! But you're making a major mistake in your viewpoint. Always try to see things from the reader's point of view, rather than from your own. People who read large numbers of resumes are, from experience, suspicious.

In a functional resume, you usually list your most marketable or highly prized skills first. And your special accomplishments, honors, or awards, regardless of when you acquired them.

Many supporters of functional resumes say the chronological resume makes it too easy for employers to screen you out. They say, correctly, that you'll be rejected for being too young, too old, having too much experience in one job, for not having moved up rapidly enough, and on and on. And remember that you're trying to *remove* reasons for being screened out. It shouldn't matter that you earned your B.A. in 1975 (or 1965 or whenever) rather than in 1989. Or that you learned to supervise people in 1981 rather than more recently. The question is or should be: Do you now have the skills needed to do this job well?

But before you decide to use a purely functional resume, let's look at the advantages and disadvantages of such a resume, so you can see what you're up against.

Pros And Cons Of A Functional Resume

A functional resume can do these good things for you:

- Remove emphasis on age
- Place emphasis on results
- Show skills you have and how you have used them
- Is ideal for returning-to-work housewives, mothers, students and others who haven't done paid-for work for some time
- Lets you transfer skills into results ... "old" jobs into skills that are in demand

A functional resume makes these problems for you:

- Most resumes are chronological, so yours is *different*.
- Lack of chronology may lead to the suspicion you're covering up something bad, even if you're not.
- They're more difficult to follow or read.
- It is difficult to find out the *most recent* experience, which is what most employers are willing to pay for ... and on which they may be basing salary, and so on
- Can seem devious to some readers

So put yourself in the *reader's* place and think about what type of resume will work best for you.

The Combination Resume

The combination resume combines elements of the chronological and functional resumes. It may be a solution for people who insist on avoiding an out-and-out chronological listing of the months and years they have worked at each job. Such a resume incorporates the best features of functional and chronological resumes. For many people, this is the format I suggest they consider.

Sample Combination Resume

On the next page, is a typical combination resume. It combines elements of the chronological resume and the functional or skills resume. The combination resume may be best for certain situations, even though it is slightly more difficult for readers to follow, because sections of the resume do not follow in a perfectly logical order.

Nancy B. Faraday
678 14th Street
    Apartment 1B
Louisville, Kentucky 40200
(502) 555-3386 (home)
(502) 555-6244 (answering service)

Job Objective: Manufacturer's Representative, Consumer Products

SALES EXPERIENCE

- Responsible for company's drapery marketing activities in four-state territory (Oklahoma, Kansas, Missouri & Arkansas). Established brand new territory; made all sales calls and contacts for $20-million manufacturer and distributor of draperies sold to multi-family apartment housing industry.

- Consistently ranked in top 5 of 14-person drapery sales force (other eight territories were established). Sales averaged $75,000 monthly (four states).

- Active in six local clubs and organizations for professional real estate and property management.

- Sold, designed, programmed and installed new electronic point-of-purchase cash record systems for retail use (stores, restaurants, malls, offices). Opened and successfully managed new territory in northern suburbs of Atlanta.

- Exceeded monthly sales quotas by average of 35% in Atlanta territory. New customers accounted for 75% of sales. Awarded incentive trip to Mexico.

- As District Manager for Florida and Georgia Region, increased sales for Chicago-based manufacturer of small appliances 71% over prior year. Cited by manager for "outstanding performance and results."

WORK HISTORY

- Hart's Mills Draperies, Atlanta, Georgia, 1988-Present

- Electronix Cash Systems, Atlanta, Georgia, 1984-1988

- General Appliances, Chicago, Illinois, 1982-1984

EDUCATION

- Bachelor of Science Degree in Business Administration Northern Illinois University, DeKalb, Illinois, 1984
- Graduate studies, Computer Programming, M.B.A., Georgia State University, Atlanta, 1986-1987

The Basics Of A Good Resume

No matter what type of resume you decide to use, you'll need a lot of time to do your best resume. One draft won't do it! In fact, it may take four or five drafts to complete a resume you'll be proud to send out. You must edit, edit, edit . . . down to a manageable length. You need to tailor it to what the reader wants to read, rather than saying everything you'd love to say about yourself.

Design For Readability

No matter how well-qualified you may be, the design and readability of your resume will be most important to the reader. The design: the look and the graphics of your resume will determine whether your resume will be **read** at all. That's the purpose of this book. There are many resume books on the market. This one is designed to show you how to have the **best** resume possible, based on content, design, and readability.

Finally, I want you to be invited to an interview and to be offered the job you want! This book—and your new resume—will help!

Chapter 2
Collecting Your Thoughts

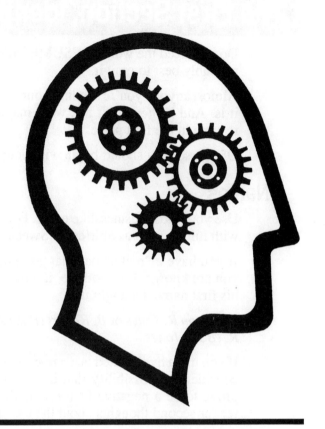

Collect, Organize, And Categorize

Before you begin considering design and readability—the basis for your successful resume—you need to collect the "raw material" of your life. This chapter will help you organize your history into useful categories for resume writing. They are:

- Identification
- Career objective
- Areas of effectiveness
- Work experience
- Education

- School activities
- Community activities
- Personal data
- Special Skills
- References

In this chapter and the next, I will guide you in completing each of these sections for use in your resume. This will be basic, unedited material, so don't try to put it in final form yet. Later, it will form the basis for your resume content.

Now, you can begin to begin! Complete each section in pencil (which will allow you to make changes), following the instructions. This is important work, but it is easy. So if you want to complete it while listening to music or watching light TV, you might find the task more enjoyable.

The First Section, Identification

Do you need the word "RESUME" at the top of the page? Not necessarily. It's probably best to omit it.

Almost anyone you're sending your resume to will immediately recognize what it is. And if they don't . . . well, maybe you shouldn't be sending them your resume in the first place.

Of course, you should begin with your name, placed at the top of the page.

Names

Use your most businesslike name. For most people, that will be your full name, with initial, such as Shirley A. Sweeney or B. Scott Janis.

If you have a "real name" that you neither use nor like, use the one by which you are known. For example, if a man named Buckhampton R. Jones dislikes his first name, he might use:

Hampton R. Jones or *B. Robert (Bob) Jones* or *Buck R. Jones* or *Buckhampton R. (B.R.) Jones*

If you use a hyphenated last name, such as Marita Ann Schillingworth-Gieselo, consider the possibility that in a first glance skim-through, your name may prove to be a negative factor. Any difficult-to-pronounce word might give a reader second thoughts about the ease of reading a difficult document.

If you have ever wrestled with "Shall I read this Dostoevsky novel . . . or not?" you probably picked up the heavy book and considered the names themselves in your decision. More than likely, you said, "This is going to be difficult, not something I can read lightly in my leisure time."

Why would the people who read your resume be any different? They're not. They are turned off by difficult words, including names.

So if you do have the option, use the name that makes reading easiest for the reader.

Keep It Simple

On your resume, then, you might consider using just *one* last name, the one you prefer using for business. Some people find that having a business name (a name that is easy to spell and pronounce) is valuable to them.

(Some friends of mine have complained for years, only half-seriously, about having to spell their names every time they use them, or about having them mispronounced by virtually everyone.)

A businesswoman I know, whose last name is Mule, has the informational phrase "pronounced Mool" beneath her name on her business card. I agree. This is a considerate and kind way to handle a possibly difficult problem for the recipient.

Make your name easy to understand, easy to read, and easy to pronounce. Think of the reader, not of yourself. You can easily clear up any misunderstandings or mispronunciations during your interview.

If your name is unusually complicated—has many middle names, difficult spellings, and so on—simplify it!

Should you use a middle initial? Maybe. Some people consider it stuffy and pompous. But if you have a very common last name, such as Johnson, Smith or Jones, you may wish to differentiate yourself by using your middle name or your middle initial.

Middle names, too, seem a bit too much for resumes, unless you need the extra name to eliminate the possibility that two people with the same name are applying for the job.

Now, write your name here—in the most acceptable way—to create the best impression for yourself:

(First Name)	(Middle Initial or Name)	(Last Name)

Address

Use the best-sounding address you have, without abbreviations (which make reading/skimming more difficult, not less!).

If you have a post office box, consider using your "real" address instead. A house number is usually more impressive and substantial-sounding than a post office box.

If your address is correctly written:

    1567 Wilson Terrace (rear cottage)

consider eliminating the (rear cottage) portion. And if you have two addresses, your permanent address and your school address, you may want to use both.

Here are some examples:

• Margaret Samuels-Berlinsky 7755 Colorado Circle Dayton, Ohio 45472-8813	• John Malchow 5775 Columbus Street Odessa, Texas 72241-1648
• Barton E. Commerly Apartment #308 1455 N. 86th Street New York, New York 10744-4346	• Lucille Weyker 2254 Ludington Terrace San Diego, California 90277-6862

Something To Think About

The name of your city or home town says something about you, your personality, and about the ways in which prospective employers may perceive you. Such judgments and opinions may not be fair, but they do exist.

For example, if you are asked "Where are you from?" when visiting Europe, and you say, "Chicago," the response will likely be "Oh! Gangster! Bang-bang!"

If, on the other hand, you say "Northern Illinois, where there are many farms," you will be perceived differently.

If you list Beverly Hills as your address, you'll get a slightly different reaction than if you say Los Angeles.

The new 9-digit ZIP code enables the post office to deliver mail to your home or building, without further identification on an envelope. So if you list your 9-digit ZIP code, you may have a bit of latitude in naming the city in which you live.

Therefore, you may accurately say that you live in Milwaukee, Wisconsin, when you actually live in the neighboring village of Sussex, which is "out in the country," and which your reader may not recognize.

The reader will probably know where Milwaukee is, however. And she may also imagine you have a more sophisticated personality if your home address is in a city of 25,000 or 30,000, or 500,000 or more, rather than an unknown suburb.

Obviously, if you live in a small town, with no city nearby, you will give the name of your town and the correct ZIP code. The 9-digit ZIP code is now preferred in all business situations.

If you do not yet know your 9-digit ZIP code, a call to your local postmaster will usually bring you the answer in a few minutes.

Telephone Number

Give the area code and number where you may be reached most of the time.

If you are difficult to reach, you should have an answering machine. Use a businesslike message, not a Bette Davis voice or Jack Benny comedy skit! Then the prospective employer can leave a message without having to call back a dozen times in futile efforts to reach you.

If you're hard to reach by phone, the employer may well decide to give up after an attempt or two, just as you would do.

If you like, you can list (immediately below your own number) an *alternative* number, where messages will be taken for you.

Be careful, however, to get permission from the people who will be taking your messages. And let them know the circumstances: Prospective employers will be calling to leave messages, and accuracy is *very* important.

You wouldn't want to call the wrong number or mispronounce a name given to you in error. Sometimes, well-meaning friends don't do well "under fire."

A Word Of Advice

Be *extremely* careful about the persons you select to take messages for you.

If your prospective employer calls that number and hears a sloppy, unintelligible voice which answers, "Yeah, who d'ya wanna talk to?" . . . your prospective employer has every right to question your judgment or your choice of friends.

When calling a semifinalist for employment with the corporation for which I served as Corporate Director of Human Resources, the candidate's spouse answered.

The answering voice was very unprofessional, not businesslike, and there was excessive noise in the background: television and kids crying.

Prospective employers deserve a better impression of any candidate than this. Be careful. Or you may be rejected for reasons you never considered or which you thought would never count against you!

Here are some samples of the ways you might want to write your phone number:

(502) 555-1546	(work)	(601) 555-4444	(home)
(502) 807-2116	(home)	(601) 711-6512	(parents' home, messages)
(409) 555-1212	(home)	(212) 555-6401	(home)
(409) 311-4400	(spouse's)	(212) 607-4400	(answering service) (business phone)

Considering all of the above advice, write your own name, address and phone number in the spaces below. Write it just as you want it to appear on your resume. Remember, no abbreviations, and include your 9-digit ZIP code too:

_____

_____

_____

Now, write your phone number(s), with area code, here:

```
        ( _____ ) _____ - _____
        area code          number

        ( _____ ) _____ - _____
        area code          number
```

Job Objective

Including a Job or Career Objective on your resume is a controversial topic.

If you use an objective, experts will tell you that you must be specific . . . say exactly what you do or what you're looking for. True!

But what if you have a *first-choice* career objective and would gladly accept a second-choice job, or even a third or fourth choice? If you list your first choice only, you will almost certainly be eliminated from consideration for any other opportunities.

So here's what I recommend:

If you know what you want to do, very specifically, write a job or career objective. Stick to it. Hang in there. You'll get what you want eventually.

Don't Be Vague

But if you don't know what you want to do, don't write an objective at all.

You're better off not having one than having a vague, poorly-written objective. Don't expect employers to be impressed with generalities; they won't be.

And neither will employers be able to make your career decisions for you. That's not their job. It's yours.

A competent, college-degreed professional wrote the following job objective at the top of the resume:

> *A challenging opportunity with a forward-looking organization, in one or more of the following areas—marketing, management, distribution, public relations, or personnel.*

What's wrong? Too many options. This candidate looks indecisive.

Another college graduate wrote this:

> *A challenging opportunity in management.*

Sorry, fellow. You lose. This says *nothing*, other than "I don't know *what I want!*" *It was written by a 45-year old college graduate with over 15 years of business experience. He should have known better, but didn't.*

His objective is simply too broad, too general, and meaningless. It hurts the applicant, rather than helping him.

Most employers want to fill a specific job that requires specific skills. You really can't expect them to figure out the job for which you are qualified.

Your job objective, then, must also be specific. It should let the reader know, immediately, what job you are looking for. It should imply the types of problems you can *solve* and let them know that "you're the one"—or, at the very least, that you deserve further consideration.

Make Headlines

Think of a job objective as a headline. It will attract the reader, or it will not.

If your job objective says, in a few short words, that you will be able to solve one of the problems that exists in the organization, your chances are *good* for avoiding immediate rejection.

If it says *nothing* or if it is vague, too long, or seems indecisive, you're *out*. You're rejected in a 3-second glance—based on a job or career objective *alone*, before the reader even *sees* the body of your resume!

Here are some short, well-written job/career objectives:

- General Sales Manager for Machine Tool Manufacturer
- Stockbroker
- Entry-level Position in Soft Goods Retailing
- Training Program in Retailing/Marketing Management
- Assistant Buyer for Giftware
- Auto Mechanic
- Auto Mechanic for Porsche-Audi Cars
- Travel Agent In Agency Using SABRE System
- Housekeeper/Supervisor for Hotel or Motel
- Life Insurance Sales/Investment Counselor
- Assistant Loan Officer, Savings & Loan Association or Bank
- Mechanical Engineering Position with Manufacturing Firm
- Sales Representative, Floor Covering Retailer
- Territorial Sales Representative Appliance Distributor/Wholesaler
- Incentive/Premium Sales Representative
- Marketing Firm in Midwest
- Editorial Assistant in Sports-related Publishing
- Executive Secretary/Administrative Assistant
- Word Processing Supervisor

Now, write your own job objective, based on the skills you have and want to use on the job:

_____

_____

_____

_____

_____

_____

_____

Education

If you are a recent graduate (of a university, college, career or business college, vocational school, community college, or any other substantial program), education *probably* belongs near the top of your resume.

This is especially true if the courses you studied have a direct relationship to the career you hope to enter.

But if you graduated years ago, or if your educational background does not relate to your present goals, you may wish to list education items near the end of your resume.

Some of the examples that follow include more than the basics: they also include statements about courses taken, accomplishments and extracurricular activities. This can be a good idea unless you decide to list this information elsewhere in your resume.

Here are some examples of recent college graduates:

> • **Bachelor of Arts Degree**
> St. Olaf's College (Northfield, Minnesota)
> Majors: Psychology and English
> Grade Point Average: 3.85/4.0
> Graduated "Magna Cum Laude" June, 19XX
>
> • **Bachelor of Science Degree in Business Administration**
> University of Georgia
> Athens, Georgia
> Date of Graduation: May, 19XX
>
> If you have an advanced degree, list it first:
>
> • **Master's Degree in Guidance and Counseling**
> University of Southern California
> Los Angeles, California
> Graduation: December, 19XX
> Graduated with honors while working full time. Includes
>   one year practicum with a variety of clients.
> Degree granted: June 19XX
>
> • **Master of Business Administration**
> The Kellogg School, Northwestern University
> Evanston, Illinois
> Upper 25 percent of Class, Started a student service business while going to school. Earned enough to pay tuition and expenses.
> Degree Granted: June, 19XX
>
> Examples of Career or Technical School graduates:
>
> • **Associate Degree in Electronics and Computer Science**
> Computer Institute of Pittsburgh
> Pittsburgh, Pennsylvania
> Date of Graduation:
>   December, 19XX
> Grade Average: 3.65/4.0
>
> Courses include
>   Calculus, physics
>   AF & RF Analog Electronics
>   Circuit Design & Fabrication
>   Digital Electronics
>   Microprocessors

Playing The Grade Game

What if you didn't do well in school? Must you put the information about education at the top? Must you admit to your low grades?

Of course not. The resume is a sales document, and if you use it correctly, it gets you *in*. It doesn't keep you *out*.

So you say those things that will make you look like a good candidate. If you have good grades, you list them. If not, omit them.

- **Acme Diesel Training Schools**
  Completed 2-year training program
  Certificate granted:
  December, 19XX
  Grade Average: A- to B+
    Program included 12 months of on-the-job experience under the supervision of an experienced heavy duty diesel mechanic.

- **Institute of Business Careers**
  One year program in Executive Secretary and Business Management Certificate of Achievement, Leadership Award
  Graduate June, 19XX
  Courses Include:
    Computerized Accounting
    Office Management
    Business Communications
    Advanced Word Processing Systems & Procedures
    Time Management

Here are some ways to present your high school experience:

- **Shawnee Mission East High School**
  Prairie Village, Kansas
  Graduated with Honors June, 19XX
  College Preparatory Classes:
  GPA 3.8/4.0
- **Denver Vocational High School**
  Denver, Colorado
  Business Courses in accounting, word processing, data entry
    management and others
  Date of Graduation: June, 19XX

- **Storm Lake Area High School**
  Storm Lake, Minnesota
  Class of 19XX: Active in varsity sports, class president
- **Edina High School**
  Edina, California
  Graduated with Honors
  June, 19XX
  Elected to student government council twice

Or state that you "Received excellent grades in mathematics, drafting, and mechanics courses." Will the reader recognize that you are also omitting information about the poor grades you received in English Composition courses?

Possibly. But if your grades in significant courses were better than your overall average, you may prefer to use such a statement anyway.

If you have been out of school for many years, your grades are far less important than your performance in the jobs you have held.

If you want a dividing line to help you decide whether to include your grade point average (your GPA), choose 3.0 on a 4.0 system.

On the 4.0 system, the most common system used for grading in high schools and colleges in the United States, each A grade is given a weight of 4 points; a B receives 3 points, a C is 2 points, and a D is 1 point.

Someone who has all B's would have a 3.0 grade average; a straight A student would have a 4.0 average.

Is a 2.5 grade average bad? No. But it is not good enough to include as a *plus* factor in a resume.

Winning The Grade Game

In my ten years as a college placement director, almost *every* student who graduated found a job he or she wanted after graduation. But the easiest way I could sell a student to an employer was to say that he or she "has a 3.8 grade average."

Good grades are an almost certain ticket to getting in the door for an interview. The lower your grades or the poorer your record, the more doors you may have to knock on to get a chance at the job you want.

And the harder you'll have to work to make an impression in the interview.

If students only knew how much good grades impress prospective employers, they would surely put more effort toward achieving better grades.

I've never heard a mediocre student say that he or she had "done my very best work all the time." Almost invariably, they say, instead, that "I know I could have done better if I had worked harder."

(If you are reading this in time to make a difference in your grades and make a change in your habits—*do it now*!)

Listing Your Educational Experience

Here are some tips before you begin.

List the names of all the schools from which you graduated, beginning with your high school. If you did not graduate, list the last school you attended and the year in which you would have graduated, such as "Class of 1989."

If you attended four high schools, list only the one from which you received your diploma. The same is true for colleges and universities. List the one from which you graduated or the school you attended most recently.

Most colleges and high schools include you as an alumnus (male) or alumna (female), even if you did not graduate. Employers are interested in just knowing that you *did* attend or that you *did* graduate.

They are not as interested in knowing each school you may have attended while moving from city to city, or while changing your mind about what subjects to study.

Here, as elsewhere in your resume, do not use abbreviations. Spell out the names of organizations—even streets and locations, and spell them correctly. Begin by completing the following form for your most recent educational experience.

Most Recent Educational Experience

School name: _____

Location (city & state): _____

Note: Street addresses, ZIP codes and phone numbers are not required here. Be prepared to provide this information, if asked, to an employer needing to check your references or credentials.

Degree/Diploma/Certificate awarded, if any:_____

_____

Month and year of graduation: _____

Courses that directly relate to the job you are seeking: _____

_____

_____

_____

_____

_____

Class rank: I ranked _____ in a class of _____ graduating students.

I had a grade average of _____ out of a possible _____. [and/or]

I had a grade average of _____ in my major subjects of study, out of a possible _____.

Special skills you acquired, accomplishments, honors, projects, extracurricular or related activities: _____

_____

_____

_____

_____

_____

Note: Use additional sheets of paper as needed to list all your related activities and accomplishments. But, before you write your resume, select out the top few things you feel are most important for an employer to know.

_____

_____

_____

_____

_____

Now, for each school you attended or from which you graduated, list the information required on the form that follows.

School Information

School name: _____

Location (city & state):_____

_____

Degree/Diploma/Certificate awarded, if any:_____

_____

Month and year of graduation: _____

Courses that directly relate to the job you are seeking: _____

_____

_____

_____

_____

_____

Class rank: I ranked _____ in a class of _____ graduating students.

I had a grade average of _____ out of a possible _____. [and/or]

I had a grade average of _____ in my major subjects of study, out of a possible _____.

Special skills you acquired, accomplishments, honors, projects, extracurricular or related activities: _____

_____

_____

_____

_____

There you have it. A record of your educational experiences.

In the next chapter, I will show you the sections of a resume that *really* get the attention of most employers.

Chapter 3
Tell 'Em What Sells 'Em

Your past experiences are the most important part of your resume. An employer is going to pay you for these experiences, in the hope that it will directly translate into skills valuable to the employer.

Past experiences indicate how you are likely to perform in the future. So you'll want to present your strongest experiences in a clear and powerful way.

Why Are They Looking To Hire You—Or Anyone?

When anyone buys something, they are often buying more than the product or service itself. They buy the *benefits,* the specific features, advantages and attributes which the product or service will bring to them.

When you buy a television, for example, you are buying more than the hardware. You are buying:

- Design
- Convenience features (remote channel changing, etc.)

- Reputation for quality and reliability
- Picture quality
- Lifestyle benefits

Charles Revlon, the famed founder of the Revlon cosmetics empire, was fond of saying, "I don't sell cosmetics, I sell hope." In a similar way an employer, too, buys the *benefits* a job applicant brings to the organization.

You'll want to pay special attention, then, to the ways you can best communicate your skills, talents, abilities, and aptitudes that you can bring to an organization . . . the *benefits* you offer.

The more benefits you bring, and the fewer potential problems, the more likely you are to be screened *in* and not screened *out*.

In your resume, the best way to accomplish this is *to do what most people neglect to do:*

- Emphasize your *accomplishments*, and
- Tell the reader any *specific results* you have had.

This is far better than listing the "duties and responsibilities of the job," which is what most people do in resumes.

They fail to *market* themselves. Employers buy *results, accomplishments, and benefits*. So, that's what you should put in your resume!

What Are Accomplishments?

Accomplishments are things you started, completed, worked on, created, developed or made possible . . . things that happened because *you* were there!

An accomplishment can be a long or short term project, something created or supervised by others, or by yourself.

But they are always specific, not general, and they are always things in which you played an active role (even if others worked with you.)

Look at the difference between a duty (which does *not* market you effectively but is the way most people write their resumes) and the same situation described as an accomplishment:

A duty:

> **Wrote weekly reports on sales and submitted these to home office.**

An accomplishment:

> **Completed 156 summary reports on sales, including weekly volume, percent of increase, new clients seen. Received commendation from sales manager for accuracy and for never missing a deadline.**

Which, do you think, will impress an employer more?

What About Results?

Doing something is one thing; doing it well is quite a different thing. Results detail the positive differences, advantages and changes which occurred as a consequence of your efforts. They are best expressed in easy to understand words or in numbers.

When writing your resume, select the statistics which *best* show the results you have achieved and, therefore, the kinds of results you are capable of achieving for an employer.

Here is an "ordinary" result (*not* a good example):

> *Sold complete line of cars and trucks for a major metropolitan dealer for six years. Interfaced with sales force, customers, service department; prospected by phone.*

Now, look at how this same experience can be changed into a *good* statement:

- Member, 'Winner's Circle,' honors sales club for Goodman Chevrolet, 1987-1989.
- Sold 200+ new cars and 50+ new trucks annually—over $2,500,000 in sales—for each of the past four years.
- Received dealer's highest measured customer rating for most of the 70 months on sales force.
- Averaged 50 cold call phone contacts daily, converting 6 percent into customers.
- Contacted "prior dealership customers" list by phone and set new sales records with this previously ignored group.

Which of these descriptions would impress you the most?

Analyze Your Work Experience

Your previous work experience is an important source of resume content. More recent experience is of greater importance than examples from years ago.

If you are young, or if your previous jobs are unrelated to your current objective, the *type* of experience you have is not all that important to most employers.

Employers are more interested in the fact that you worked somewhere, that you are ambitious, that you worked hard and did a good job than they are in what sort of job you had—unless it has a very specific relationship to the job you are seeking.

But your advancement at McDonald's to supervisor or your ability to train new staff could well add to your attractiveness as a candidate with virtually any employer.

And so could the fact that you supervised six employees. Or that you earned 80 percent of your schooling expenses while maintaining a B average.

So whether you are 20 and just starting out or 45 with considerable work experience, you want your resume to show off your accomplishments in the best possible light.

So, let's get on with it.

The Basics: Selling Your Work Experience

I have constructed a worksheet later in this section to help organize your work experiences. Here are some tips for completing it.

The Organization. For each employer, write the full name of the company (spelled correctly) and the city and state where it is located.

Title. Write your job title. If your job title is difficult to understand or if it doesn't mean anything by itself, change it!

- Change "Sales Associate" to "Senior Retail Sales Clerk, Men's Clothing Department," if that is appropriate.
- Change "Secretary" to "Office Manager," if that description is more accurate.

City and State/Province. If the job was located in a suburb of a major city, it is OK to use that city's name.

Length of Employment. Give the month and year you began, and the month and year that you left. If you are still employed there, write "present" in the appropriate place.

Results and Accomplishments. Write *short* statements of specific results and accomplishments you had on this job.

Use Action Words

Begin each statement with an action verb. Use words or ideas from the "Action Words" list that follows to make sure you begin each phrase with an action word.

Write each statement as a *phrase*, not a *sentence*.

Action Words List

• Accomplished	• Maintained	• Led	• Established
• Initiated	• Conducted	• Compiled	• Reported
• Achieved	• Managed	• Made	• Persuaded
• Inspected	• Constructed	• Composed	• Planned
• Adjusted	• Mixed	• Created	• Determined
• Instructed	• Controlled	• Operated	• Prepared
• Judged	• Motivated	• Cut	• Developed
• Built	• Moved	• Organized	• Presented
• Justified	• Counseled	• Designated	• Devised
• Directed	• Promoted	• Fabricated	• Figured

Action Words List

• Evaluated	• Revised	• Served	• Sold
• Researched	• Exhibited	• Drove	• Enlarged
• Entertained	• Reorganized	• Equipped	• Replaced
• Graded	• Guided	• Handled	• Headed
• Supervised	• Taught	• Tended	• Trained
• Protected	• Encouraged	• Recorded	• Reduced
• Implemented	• Won	• Improved	• Wrote
• Compared	• Negotiated	• Administered	• Produced
• Increased	• Invented	• Analyzed	• Interviewed
• Designed			

Omit these three words from your writings: "I," "me," and "my." Then omit three more: "a," "an," and "the." These are "extra" words, and they are not particularly appropriate for resume-style writing. Your phrases will be cleaner, shorter, and easier to understand if you omit these words.

Describe each accomplishment separately. If you think about it, you may be able to separate one project into several smaller skills or accomplishments. This can give you shorter (and more powerful) statements, rather than a description of one big project.

Keep each accomplishment short, so that it can be read *quickly* by the reader!

Use numbers whenever you can—exact numbers or percentages are powerful.

And if you had several jobs or accomplishments that sound the same, *do not* repeat the same thing for each job or department in which you worked. This should be obvious but I have seen it hundreds of times!

Here are some examples of "good" statements:

- Wrote 300+ programs for IBM main frame computer system
- Received seven letters of commendation from sales executives for exceeding quotas.
- Increased sales 41 percent over prior year for same territory. Established 77 new accounts.
- Implemented new sales record system, saving 4 hours weekly for each sales representative, or total of 128 weekly hours, which were then available for sales calls.
- Managed sales force of 36 independent agents and 22 company sales representatives, covering seven fields and 29 territories.
- Reduced inventories 17 percent by developing and implementing new sales forecasting system
- Reformulated 13 cereal and snack products to conform with federal guidelines for shelf-life improvement.

- Reformulated non-dairy topping product for improved taste. Decreased cost of raw materials by $150,000 annually.

- Invented and patented new method of treating perishable food products. Reduced annual cost of formulation by more than $250,000 per year.

- Negotiated and sold injection molding division for parent company. Resulted in $3,000,000 profit; saved plant shutdown costs estimated at $170,000.

- Supervised 7 full-time and 18 part-time retail sales employees.

- Won 14 design awards for graphic design of three metals-industry magazines published for nationwide distribution.

- Developed new typesetting system using MS-DOS computer system when software was not available to meet company's needs.

- Won ADDY Award for excellence in creativity for full-page newspaper advertisement. National award was won by only 3 people from 7,000 entries.

Do this for *each* job you have held. It may seem like a great deal of work, but do it in a relaxed environment, while watching TV or listening to your favorite relaxing music, and the words will come quickly.

Use additional sheets of paper to describe your various jobs as needed, using the worksheet that follows:

Work Experience Worksheet

Employer: _____

Job Title: _____

Address: _____

_____

Employed from: (month/ year) _____ to: (month/ year) _____

Results & Accomplishments: _____

_____

_____

_____

_____

_____

_____

_____

_____

_____

Work Experience Worksheet

Employer: _____

Job Title: _____

Address: _____

_____

Employed from: (month/ year) _____ to: (month/ year) _____

Results & Accomplishments: _____

_____

_____

_____

_____

_____

_____

_____

_____

After You Have Documented Your Work Experience

After you have completed a worksheet for each of your jobs, decide which *one* result or accomplishment was *most* important. Which would look *best* to a future employer?

Rank that one #1. Choose the next most important. Rank it #2. And so on.

If you did the same things on each of your last several jobs, do this: For the jobs you held years ago, write shorter job/results/accomplishments paragraphs than you write for more recent jobs.

Reword the group of related asscomplishiments to sound slightly different, and use shorter statements. If some results (expressed in numbers, percentages) and increases are significant, be sure to include some of these in your statements.

Generally, the more recent your job, the more space it should receive on your resume. Jobs you held 10, or more, years ago are usually *considerably* less significant.

If these "older" jobs do not relate at all to the job you are now seeking, they deserve only a line or two. Mention them primarily to show where you were working and for how long.

You will see, when you finish writing each statement, that some are more important than others. And that some relate more directly to the work you want now.

This process will help you to begin thinking about which items to include in your final resume, and which ones to eliminate.

For most people, the work experience section of their resume is the most important. You are hired for the *results* you have had on your jobs, for your *accomplishments*, and for your *ability* to *solve employer problems*.

In the statements in this section, you are explaining why you will be a valuable employee. The reader is more likely to consider you favorably because of these statements than from anything else in your resume.

This is generally true *unless* you are relatively young.

For most young people, "meaningful work, related to what you want to do for a career" is difficult to find. So don't be discouraged if this section, for you, is filled with results and accomplishments from your after-school grocery-bagging experiences, your baby-sitting jobs, and such.

These jobs still give employers an idea of your accomplishments, of the responsibilities you have been given, and of any promotions you have earned, and awards you have won.

Personal Accomplishments

There is more to life than work. Many times, things you have accomplished outside of work can be just as impressive to an employer as work-related activities. These can be particularly important if you have only limited work experience.

Complete the following sections for each period in your life to help review this part of your experience.

High School. List any clubs, societies, athletic or other organizations you were involved in and any awards or accomplishments for them.

_____

_____

_____

_____

_____

_____

_____

_____

18-22 years old. List any clubs, societies, athletic or other organizations you were involved in and any awards or accomplishments for them.

_____

_____

_____

_____

_____

_____

22-25 years old. List any clubs, societies, athletic or other organizations you were involved in and any awards or accomplishments for them.

_____

_____

_____

_____

_____

_____

25 years old and above. List any clubs, societies, athletic or other organizations you were involved in and any awards or accomplishments for them.

_____

_____

_____

_____

_____

_____

Choose Your Most Impressive Results

Now, from all these, choose the *most* impressive results and accomplishments you have had in your extracurricular, community, and social life.

Choose significant items, just as you did when you listed accomplishments from your work experiences.

Place #1 alongside the most impressive or significant item. Do the same for #2, #3, and so forth.

Now, in order, list the extracurricular statements in the following spaces. Again, use the action language you used when you wrote about your work accomplishments.

Here are some examples for you to follow:

- Elected President of Student Council for 1700-student high school by widest margin in school history

- Developed and chaired project to raise $4,500 for school veterans' memorial

- Elected Captain, swim team; won four varsity letters; set two team speed records

- Elected Secretary-Treasurer of Girls' Athletic Association 2 consecutive years

- Represented church youth group at national delegate convention; served on Credentials Committee

- Worked at several restaurants part-time during high school and college; earned 75 percent of college expenses

- Selected as female romantic lead for three high school musicals; received excellent reviews from local papers

- Received Regional Musical Awards for piano; studied piano privately for nine years; choir accompanist

- Elected Honored Queen, Bethel #6, Job's Daughters; increased membership 27 percent during term of office 1986-87.

- Selected for membership, Rotary Club of Downtown Phoenix, 1987. Plan to serve on education and scholarship committees.

- President, Scottsdale Jaycees, 1985-86; raised $8,000 for Special Olympics.

- Elected Lieutenant Governor, Arizona Boys State, 1968; led legislative session.

How many of these "Honors, Awards and Achievements" should you include? Some people, even some "resume experts" might say that you should omit them entirely.

I disagree.

If a potential employer is in doubt about a possible candidate, these achievements might be the very thing that would tilt the odds in your favor.

Indeed, a study of corporate personnel representatives who recruit graduating seniors on college campuses showed that participation in activities, offices, and organizations indicated that *leadership potential* was the #1 reason for choosing final candidates.

Now, in order, list the honors, awards, and achievements you want to include in your resume:

_____   _____

_____   _____

_____   _____

_____   _____

_____   _____

Think Again

If you don't have any activities, honors, awards, or extracurricular accomplishments, don't feel left out.

First, you probably *do* have some. Think again. Think about how you may have spent your free time. Think about a boss who may have paid you a special compliment about your work, your effort, or your dependability.

You might include this in a section rarely used, but possibly useful:

What Others Say

A short, swift compliment may be just the thing to compensate for your lack of "honors." If your boss once said that you were her best employee, use the words she said.

> *Best employee I've ever had in fourteen years of hiring high school students.*
>
> —Linda Keeler, Manager, 7-11 Store, East Dubuque

Or if a teacher once said that your assignments were always handed in on time, repeat that teacher's words:

> *I admire your neat work and the fact that you always have assignments in on time.*
>
> —Allen B. Molitor, Teacher, American History, Darien High School

If you use quotes, be sure they are accurate! And keep quotations short. One phrase or sentence is usually enough! You want employers to read it, absorb it, then generalize from it.

What you want them to remember is:

> *He seems like a good person, and other people seem to think so, too.*

Special Skills

This is the place to list any special skills not already covered in your Work Experience or Education sections. Such skills might include typing, operating specific machinery and equipment, and so on.

Make a list of any special skills you might have that would interest an employer. And mark the ones that you want to use in a job.

Because maybe you can type but would rather not let employers know this (for fear of being labeled a secretary—when you really want to be a management trainee).

There's no law that says you must use *all* your skills in a job. Or admit to them on a resume.

List any of these skills in the following spaces.

_____

_____

_____

_____

_____

_____

Personal Information

In years past, this information was expected. People who were reading resumes looked for it. But times change, and so do resume customs.

Omit information such as date of birth or age, place of birth, family information, marital status, health, height, and weight.

Put in anything here that might help you, and leave out anything that could hurt you. Although this section can be left off your resume completely, it *might* be helpful to include some things that do support your ability to do the job but don't fit anywhere else on your resume.

Condition of your health, in one word:_____.

(I recommend the word "excellent.")

Have you traveled much? Where? List the unusual or interesting regions, states, or foreign countries you've visited:

_____

_____

_____

_____

_____

Have you had any special training, professional schooling, attended intensive seminars, gone to service/military schools which are applicable to the civilian job you're hoping to land?

List them here, including the length of each course.

_____

_____

_____

_____

_____

_____

What are your hobbies? Interests? List them here. (Some ideas: playing baseball, composing classical music for piano, collecting first day stamp issues, reading about current business trends, making your own clothes, working on cars, skydiving, parasailing, writing movie reviews for local paper, eating out, seeing foreign films, volunteering at local nursing home, assisting Sunday School teachers, 35mm photography, scripting and videotaping original variety shows, building bookcases, making needlepoint pictures, etc.)

_____

_____

_____

_____

Now, start looking at, and thinking about, which ones of the above you would like to have a prospective employer know about? Which ones might make you look more attractive to an employer? Which ones would not?

Some kinds of personal information can cause problems. In most cases, your resume should be free of references to your political, religious, or philosophical beliefs.

An exception to this general rule might be when you are applying to a religious, political, or philosophical organization. Degrees from religious colleges or universities, therefore, might be helpful if you are applying to work at a hospital run by that religion. People of all religions may work there, of course, but you might have a slight advantage.

Political preferences are no reason for selecting one applicant over another. Your beliefs are your own business as long as you don't try to force them on other employees in the organization.

But listing that you were a member of the Young Democrats when the chances are 50-50 that the reader will be a Republican, wouldn't seem to be a smart idea. You'd be better off to eliminate the reference entirely. Or, you might say "Elected President of political organization with membership of 80" rather than identifying the Young Democrats specifically.

Use this as a guideline: if you feel any of this personal information is to your advantage in the job hunt, you *may* use it if you wish.

I recommend a short statement, under a category titled "PERSONAL INFOR-MATION," very close to the end of your resume, if you use it at all. Here are some examples:

- Excellent health, no serious illnesses
- Middle child of five children; father is airline sales representative; mother is office manager for plumbing firm
- Married to Ralph, computer engineer, for 27 years; raised five children
- Have traveled widely throughout United States, Canada and Europe; enjoy travel photography
- Enjoy sewing clothes, church committees, volunteer work at nursing home

References

References are not usually listed on a resume.

A resume is one of the first things an employer sees in the hiring process; reference calls and inquiries aren't made until later. But you might begin, now, to think about which people you would choose to recommend you, to inform the prospective employer about things such as your trustworthiness, honesty, dependability, work diligence and habits, your career goals, the quality of your work, and even the kinds of friends you have.

The best choices for references are usually, but need not always be, people who have watched you work, supervised your work, instructed you, graded you, who have seen you progress to new levels of competence, etc. Who are these people? Usually your teachers, bosses, supervisors, owners of businesses or executives of organizations where you have worked, and with whom you have had a direct working relationship.

References may be requested from others: ministers, neighbors, or your family doctor or attorney. But these are not considered as valuable by most employers. Obviously, if you were applying for a job with a church, a reference from your pastor might prove to be very important. But for a job as Administrative Assistant for the Vice President of Manufacturing, a minister's comments might not be as significant.

Put some of their names down now, and then think about how you might approach these people to ask their permission to act as a reference for you.

_____

_____

_____

_____

_____

_____

_____

_____

When you select the people to be your references, you will choose about three or four. For each of these you will need the following information:

- Full name
- Name of Organization
- Address
- City, state, zip
- Job title of the person
- Your working or personal relationship, in a few words at most
- Telephone number, including area code.

Remember, references are not required on your resume because it represents an early stage in the application process. Your goal now is to create a resume which is so attractive that you will be asked to come in for an interview. After a successful interview, if you are under final consideration as a candidate, the employer will ask for your references. If you wish to forget about references entirely, or if you hope the employer does, a simple phrase like the following will often do nicely.

> *Business and personal references are available and will be furnished on request.* or

> *Excellent business and personal references are available.* or

> *Complete business and personal references are available and will gladly be furnished on request.*

Well, you get the picture by now. Except to say that such a statement can just as easily be left off the resume entirely. Because it really says nothing.

And one other thing, *always* ask permission before using a person as a reference. Talk over what they will say in advance and use them *only* if they will say good things about you.

Letters Of Reference

Many organizations no longer give out references over the phone. They may even fear a lawsuit based on something they might say. Or they don't want to offend anyone. Supervisors sometimes leave from where you worked for other jobs. So getting a *written* letter of reference is becoming more and more important. This is the only way to be certain of getting a reference from a previous employer.

Not all references are good ones. How do you get a good reference?

From an employer's point of view, the best references are from those who can tell them the truth about your *performance*, not just that you are "a nice person."

Current and ex-bosses, current teachers and ex-teachers are probably the best people to do this. Your aunt, minister, dentists and others who know you only as a friend, client, or relative are not acceptable references to an employer.

Begin by selecting some people who know your work and who will say positive things about you. Then help them in saying what you want them to say in their letters.

Remember, employers will be looking for negative information. Faint praise in a letter of reference can be damaging. So if you're asking someone to write a letter for you, be specific. *Tell* them what to say!

Tell them to write about specific accomplishments you were involved with ... how vital your actions and results became to the organization, and so on.

Here are a few examples:

> *Amy was always dependable and always on time. She got along extremely well with her co-workers and we hate to see her resign and move away. Her work has been exceptional and we would hire her again for this job, or for a more responsible one.*

> *Bob was one of our hardest working students. He always did his homework and was active in many extracurricular activities. He did all this while working to pay his tuition . . .*

Don't be afraid to suggest improvements in the letter.

Or, if they say they'd love to give you a letter but they hate to write, offer to write something for them.

Ask them what they would say if they did write something. Then put it into words that make you sound like a trustworthy person and a good candidate.

And have them sign it if they agree with what you've said. On their letterhead. That helps convince an employer that your letters of reference are legitimate and reliable.

Offer to type the letter right away and have them sign it. Or you can draft the letter and have them type it on their letterhead right away.

If you walk out of the person's office with just their promise to write a letter "sometime soon," you may have a long wait.

Overcoming Bad References

Bad references can ruin everything! Good resumes, the perfect interview, excellent background . . . all can go down the tubes when your ex-boss says, "I wouldn't hire that guy again after what he did to me."

If you know or believe you have bad references, you have two options:

- Keep applying and hope you find someone who'll hire you without checking references at all. (Some smaller firms may not check references. Larger organizations have often been burned by hiring bad people and almost always check references to avoid being burned again.)
- Do something that turns those bad references into good ones.

This later option may be difficult. But it can be done!

Almost all wounds heal in time. It's a matter of "who eats the crow."

If it's a standoff—and both of you are unwilling to swallow your pride and make overtures to settle the hard feelings—remember *you're* the one who has the most to lose.

So YOU should take that first step toward a truce. Think of some *good* things about your ex-boss or your ex-company. Then send a letter, outlining those good things and thanking them for the good experience you had while you worked there.

Be positive. And don't reopen old wounds.

If you prefer, use the telephone instead of a letter. And say the same kinds of things.

Use truthful, positive comments and compliments . . . ones which will help the person understand that you want to patch things up and at least not be enemies from now on.

This technique often turns bad references into good ones.

And whenever you leave a job, or after you leave, do *yourself* a favor: *don't complain about anything.*

Not your boss.

Or the "rotten way" the company is run.

Or the "lousy pay" you were getting.

Smile. Swallow your pride.

Compliment your boss. And the company.

And pretend everything is wonderful.

Even if it isn't.

You'll only hurt yourself if you do otherwise. You will only make it difficult (if not impossible) to get good references when you need them.

And you *will* need them when you're looking for a job!

Using Testimonials In Your Resume

People are naturally skeptical. You may safely assume that most employers wonder if you're a "fake product" and "not likely to work after we buy your services."

One way to avoid this skepticism is to use the advertisers' favorite technique for dispelling doubt—the testimonial.

If several people are willing to tell how terrific you are, how effective a worker you are—and if these testimonials are readily available—these might turn the tide in your favor.

So, consider including testimonials in your resume! Edit them down to short punchy statements. They might be just the thing that sets you apart from your competitors.

How to get them?

- From reviews or evaluations of your work in your personnel file
- From documents, letters you have
- Letters from friends
- Letters from teachers/professors
- Letters from employers
- Letters from co-workers

If you don't have any such letters, ask for them! Consider these examples. You can include these at the beginning or end of the resume (wherever they would have the most impact):

As our night attendant for Bill's Chevron Service, Sally Kobe performed her work in an outstanding way. We entrusted her with all our equipment and gave her responsibility for making bank deposits and locking the store at 11 p.m. We were never disappointed in her and recommend her highly as a dependable, loyal employee.

—William Kozlicki, Owner

This statement could be shortened as follows:

Sally Kobe is a dependable, loyal employee.

—William Kozlicki, Owner, Bill's Chevron Service

Here are other examples:

Walter Upchuk worked for our insurance agency for three years while he attended classes at Clark County Community College. He has typed all our policy claim forms and done our company payroll and bookkeeping. His work has always been of excellent quality, and we are especially pleased with his dependability, including his attendance (he never missed a day!).

— *William Liebert, CLU, Liebert Insurance Agency*

Bill Gallant is the finest young man I've ever known. He is an excellent youth leader and sets an example for all the kids to follow. I'd like my own kids to grow up to be like Bill.

— *Jeff Parker, Director, Springfield YMCA*

Jennifer Johnson was my outstanding student this year. She did her work on time, and it was always of excellent quality. She received one of three A's I awarded, but hers was the tops in the class. I'd teach forever if all the students were like Jennifer.

— *Todd Bogwell, Assistant Professor, Midwest University*

Our Student Ambassadors are carefully selected to be the best possible representatives of the college. Among these, the best performer and worker is usually elected President. This year, it was Patrick Ryan, and Pat has outdone himself. In my memory, Pat was the best of the best.

— *Ronald Zess, Faculty Advisor*

My service station is more than my job. It is the key to my career and to my family life as well. A good employee at my station is someone who not only works for me, but whom I trust to be a good representative for the business. If I get a bad guy, my kids may not go to college. John Clark is the perfect employee: trustworthy, dependable, always neatly groomed and pleasant. My customers enjoy coming in and usually ask for John. I recommend him highly.

— *Alice Springs, Owner, Springs Service*

Do you have some testimonials like these? If not, can you get some?

From past employers? Or co-workers? Or teachers? Or friends?

If you do not have letters of reference, plan on getting them as soon as possible. If you do, summarize some of the best statements here for possible use in your resume later.

Testimonial Statements:

_____
_____
_____
_____
_____
_____
_____
_____
_____
_____
_____
_____
_____
_____
_____
_____
_____
_____

Chapter 4
Designing An Outstanding Resume

Tailor Your Resume For Excellence

Now that you've gathered information about yourself, you're ready to begin putting your resume together.

Unless you are now prepared to invest enough time to research, write, edit and then do the final copy of a resume that will make an *excellent* impression on the reader, all this work will have been in vain. Your resume is unlikely to be noticed or even glanced at, let alone read. One draft won't do it!

You will want to *tailor* your resume to what the reader *wants to read*—not necessarily what you want to say about yourself.

Too many people fail to put themselves in the reader's shoes! They see the resume as an opportunity to report everything about their history, because it makes them feel good to talk about all the things they've done.

The reader is looking for a *capsule impression* of you in a quick read-through of your resume. If you bury the essentials in a sea of words, the reader will never find them.

The Eye-Strain Approach

Here is an example of bad resume writing:

September 1989 — June 1990 SAFETY REPRESENTATIVE

Responsibilities: Coordinate and administer the safety, accident prevention, housekeeping, sanitation, and other related programs as assigned. Investigate accidents and supervise the preparation of accident reports and statistical summaries; review claims for worker's compensation. Check buildings, facilities, fire prevention systems, storage of dangerous fluids and gases, material handling equipment, etc. to ensure compliance with mandatory regulations and insurance requirements. Establish, coordinate, and maintain Company Fire Brigade. Study, plan, and formulate new and revised safety programs and rules; prepare recommendations and implement conformance with those which meet approval. Coordinate activities with Worker's Compensation Insurance Carrier. Select and approve purchase of standard manufactured safety services or design; expedite construction and installation of machine guards and point of operation safety.

If you were a busy employer, would you want to read this? Of course not!

The resume is *not* a place where you outline your job description or list every single duty you had. It is a place to highlight experiences that *will be relevant to the reader's requirements*—not to stroke your ego.

This isn't the place to say, "I'm wonderful." This is the place to highlight significant *results* and *accomplishments* from your experience.

To describe yourself in terms of the results you had on the job. The things you accomplished. The effects you had on corporate profitability or organizational effectiveness. The sales increases which you directly brought about.

In other words, the *provable* things.

To say "bright, witty and intellectually gifted" shows only that you have a good opinion of yourself.

We all need to love ourselves and be aware of our good qualities. But putting these things in a resume comes off as arrogant.

Better that the reader should conclude such things from the accomplishments you describe.

Or hear it from others when they check your references.

Edit, Edit, Edit

You will eventually edit your first draft and then edit the information down to a second draft (leaving out irrelevant information) . . . edit down to a third draft (seeking better, more powerful, *shorter* words) . . . edit down to a fourth draft (grammatical perfection) . . . and finally, a fifth draft (arrangement on the page). This will be your final pre-printer copy.

In your fifth draft, you will also decide the *order* of your categories, because you will want to highlight your *best* qualifications *early* in the resume.

Thus, if your strongest point is fifteen years' experience in the field in which you are applying for a job, your work experience will be more important than your education and should come before it.

But if you are a new graduate with little relevant experience, you will probably want to place your education before your work experience.

If you are a graduating student and a leader in clubs and athletics, but your grades aren't so good, you might want to highlight "Honors, Awards, and Achievements" within your educational background.

How Long Should Your Resume Be?

Most experts will tell you that your resume should be one page only. Or two pages at the most.

And they are probably right. Because no one wants to read more than that.

Your job is to edit, edit, edit your resume. And then edit some more. Until your resume is a manageable, tight length.

This does not mean that you should scrunch your resume into one page (or two) just because this is the rule.

I've seen resumes that are two and a half pages long (or even three) *with lots of white space* that were better (easier to read) than two-pagers with too much copy.

It's better to have a *well-designed* resume that will get *read*, even if it is longer, than a crowded resume.

But the chances are if your resume is more than two pages long, you're simply refusing to edit out irrelevant material in your background. Keep it to one or two pages, and you'll probably be safe.

The best length for your resume depends on your experience. Students and recent graduates may have little difficulty producing their resume on one page.

And even if you have many years of experience, remember that jobs from many years ago deserve little (if any) space unless they are *really* special or prestigious.

And unless they truly relate somehow to the job you're trying to get now. And if nothing else you've done since then relates to that objective.

But that would be a rare circumstance! So keep editing critically. Keep your resume short and easy to scan.

Secrets Of Readability

When you find yourself in a bookstore, you probably flip casually through a book that interests you.

Why? You want to see if it's readable. Is it a book you will be able to read . . . will *want* to read?

Is there good use of white space? Graphics? Are the paragraphs short? Or what?

For whatever reasons, this book must have looked inviting to you—*readable*. The same is true with resumes!

The first requirement of your resume is that it must be *inviting to the eye*. If it isn't, *it won't even get read!*

The potential resume reader (just like the potential book reader) looks at the following things:

- Are the sentences short? With easy/short words?
- Is there adequate spacing between lines?
- Are there many short one-sentence or two-sentence paragraphs? (If the words . . . the sentences . . . and the paragraphs are long, involved, and uninviting, no one will read them.)

Scholarly articles, academic journals, and most textbooks are written in a way that invites serious study. It takes concentration and effort to absorb the information in these kinds of writings.

Leisure writing, consumer magazine articles, newspapers, and advertising copy are written differently. Their authors know that readers of such things *will not have the time for serious study.*

So it is with your resume. You've got *one chance.*

Think now about the leisure reading *you* do. What does it *look* like? Is it difficult or is it easy?

It's *easy*. E-A-S-Y to read. Once through, and you know what you have read! That's what your resume should be.

Magazines, newspapers, and advertising copy are all written in a way (using a special format) that makes them inviting to the eye.

That format is something you already know about: C-O-L-U-M-N-S.

Write your resume in a *column* format! Why? Because it makes the resume easy to scan. And that, my friends, is all the reader wants to do with it.

So give them what they want. Give them something easy to read.

How Do You Read, Learn, And Enjoy?

Eye-brain coordination is a miraculous thing. If the eye grabs four, five, six words at a time—in a split second—the brain can put those words in order and make sense of them.

The principle of speed reading says that you can, with your finger as a pacing guide, zoom down the center of a column or a page and let your brain *grab* the words within your eye's field of vision.

The brain then sorts them into the right order almost automatically—as fast as your finger can move down that page!

When your eye must read *across* long lines of type (and especially lines with long words), more concentration is required. Your brain has to think about the meaning of long, unfamiliar words. And eye fatigue results from eye travel across long lines.

How The Eye Travels Across The Page

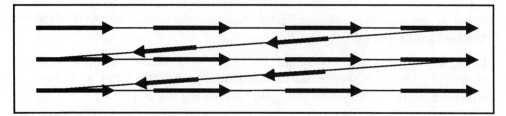

Note that the eye travels along the words in one line. Then, it must travel back across the page, right to left, and seek out the beginning of the next line.

As the eye travels first one direction, then the other, then forward again, it travels *twice the distance* you might, at first, think that it does.

The eye tires quickly. So when you look at a book to see if you might wish to purchase it, a book with "all words and very little space" looks difficult to read.

The same is true of a resume. If it contains little white space, and if it is too crowded (especially with long words), the reader gets a very negative first impression!

How Your Eyes Read A Column

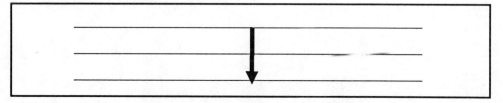

In column format, the eye goes *one* direction, *down*, and it scans all the information quickly, easily, and efficiently.

You can read *down* a column of words (with very little traveling) and let your marvelous brain do all the work! Your eyes don't get tired going all-that-distance-and-back-again.

The *marketing approach* provides openness and white space to prevent eye fatigue. It takes into account the feelings and attitudes of the "market," the person reading your resume.

The person reading the resume knows, at first glance, that this will be *easy to read*.

Even if the employer is going through a group of resumes *very quickly*, the ones that look easiest to read are likely to be given preference.

Use Columns For Eye Appeal

When using a column format, use only *one* column, not two. Any width is acceptable, as long as it is easy to read. I prefer narrow columns—ones not exceeding about 50-60 percent of a page width (about 4-5 inches on a normal page).

Think in terms of "less is better." Keep your resume clean looking, with plenty of white space if at all possible.

The reader of your resume may not have the faintest idea about what makes his or her eyes tired . . . or what makes a page readable. A resume that is easy-to-read sends the message that "This job seeker is making my job easier."

Their eyes do tell them what they (the eyes) *like* to read and what they *don't like* to read.

Keep this in mind when designing the final draft of your resume. And use *columns* to present your information. Columns *immediately* convey a message.

What message?

"You want to read *this resume* because *this one* is *easy on the eyes*.

Now, see for yourself, in this comparison, which format looks more interesting and inviting to you at a casual first glance:

A Simple Secret For Readability

(Set in 2 3/4-inch width)

Here is an example of a readable typeface, set in narrow width, for easy readability and quick scanning. If we would set this identical paragraph in a wider format, the eye would have to travel a greater distance to cover the same material, resulting in a tired feeling. Because we learn to read at an early age, and continue to read on through our lifetimes, we learn to judge quickly which paragraphs and which kinds of reading look as though they will tire us, and which kinds of reading look inviting and easy to read. Another way to improve readability is to leave the right edge of column-copy rough, or jagged, so that spaces-between-words are not excessive. If too much space is used, the result is a look of jerkiness rather than smoothness. Words which belong together, such as "Three Blind Mice," should always be placed on the same line, rather than separated on different lines. Also, use hyphens as little as possible; they add jerkiness.

Now, see how much READABILITY it loses when set in a wider, 6 and 1/2-inch format:

Here is an example of a readable typeface, set in narrow width, for easy readability and quick scanning. If we would set this identical paragraph in a wider format, the eye would have to travel a greater distance to cover the same material, resulting in a tired feeling. Because we learn to read at an early age, and continue to read on through our lifetimes, we learn to judge quickly which paragraphs and which kinds of reading look as though they will tire us, and which kinds of reading look inviting and easy to read. Another way to improve readability is to leave the right edge of column-copy rough, or jagged, so that spaces-between-words are not excessive. If too much space is used, the result is a look of jerkiness rather than smoothness. Words which belong together, such as "Three Blind Mice," should always be placed on the same line, rather than separated on different lines. Also, use hyphens as little as possible; they add jerkiness.

Be Your Own Art Director

In the advertising world, art directors are paid to *design* the page—to put each element, each bit of information in its proper location:

- So that you read the ad.
- To ensure that you read the important things first as you scan the page.
- To arouse your interest so that you will continue reading.
- And, finally, to get you to *act* on the information you have been given.

So, put yourself in the place of an art director.

You have the challenge of turning a blank piece of paper into an effective promotion piece . . . something that won't be thrown out or avoided. The message should leap out of your resume at first glance. How?

Use plenty of white space.

Don't crowd your material . . . giving the reader the impression that your resume is hard to read. It is easier to just toss your resume into the *reject pile*!

Use *design strategy* in planning your resume.

All of us learned to read from upper left to lower right. That's the way our eye naturally glides through any page.

Your resume should be designed, then, so that the eye moves down the page from upper left, down to the lower right-hand corner.

Underlining is helpful—it breaks up the monotony of a page.

(Perhaps, for example, you would like to underline *just* the names of your category headings, such as <u>WORK EXPERIENCE</u> . . . or the names of the companies/organizations for which you have worked.

Underlining aids readability, but be *consistent* throughout your resume.

Don't change margins in your resume more than necessary.

Changing margins will give your resume a *jerky* look. The look you want to achieve is *smooooooth*. Not jerky.

An exception, however, is a group of words that belong together. If you must go to a second line with a group of words, indent the second line a few spaces. This shows that these words belong with the first line.

Like this:

> *International Farm Machinery and Combine Corporation,*
> *Marketing and Distribution Division*

When describing your school or another *long* proper name, try to keep words that go together on the same line:

> *Waukesha County Technical College*
> *Pewaukee, Wisconsin*

instead of

> *Waukesha County Technical*
> *College*
> *Pewaukee, Wisconsin*

If you *must* separate some of the words in a title, *indent* the word left hanging by itself on the second line. This makes for easier understanding and leaves no question in the reader's mind about which words belong together.

Of course, for every rule there is an exception. And this rule is no exception!

After once listing the full name of an exceptionally long-named school or organization such as The Mid-State Baptist Institute for Biblical and Theological Studies, it is permissible (and preferable) to abbreviate such a name. But be sensible.

Use "Mid-State Institute" (Not MSBIBTS), because the former is easier for the reader to understand and absorb quickly. So when you write about being on that school's debate team, you could say:

> *Member, championship debate team,*
> *Mid-State Institute, 1981-82*

so long as you have previously given the full, more formal name of the institution in your resume.

Bullets are an excellent way to itemize.

Bullets are *indicators* that tell your eye to "start reading here." They can be written on your typewriter as periods. Or they can be small typewriter o's that you blacken with a felt-tip pen.

They call attention to the item and tell the eye, "Start here, eye . . . this is where you begin to read."

They also tell the reader that this line is going to be short and sweet. Not a long paragraph, but a few short items . . . each one preceded by a bullet.

You should separate bullets from the words by two or three spaces. Ad people have used this trick for ages. They still do.

You now know most of what you need to actually write and format a superior resume. In the next chapter, I will provide you with tips on how it should be "packaged."

Chapter 5

Packaging & Delivering Your Resume

Get Your Resume Noticed

If you could look through a pile of resumes on any employer's desk, what would you discover?

You'd find (even without reading a single word on a single resume) that most resumes have no *class*.

They're on cheap white paper.

Or they're handwritten.

Or they're done on an ordinary typewriter.

Or they're badly reproduced.

Do you want to be ordinary? To be a carbon copy? Of course not!

Again, put yourself in the reader's place. Think about all those *other* resumes, and convince yourself that yours has to be *so classy* that it will be *number one* in any stack of also rans.

You can't see your competition—can't tell who you are up against—but you know that *you* have to be *number one*. *Number two loses* when there's only one job!

When you have worked through to the final draft of your resume (carefully worded, edited, shortened, containing action verbs, results, and accomplishments), you have to consider your resume's final form.

Reproducing Your Resume

Now that you have your resume in its final (and *perfect*) form, you are ready to have it reproduced.

Usually, you will want to have a quantity of resumes, not just one or two. Even if you have prepared your resume for one specific use or person or organization, you may want to keep extras for your personal file. Or, you may need another copy before your resume has become outdated.

The cost of reproducing your resume will vary according to the method you select, where you live, and how many copies you desire.

In most cases, you will prepare a final draft or a *camera-ready* copy, from which any quantity may be reproduced.

If you have access to a computer, word processor, or to an electronic typewriter with a memory, you may be able to keep your entire resume *on disk* or in other storage media for later use whenever you need a copy.

But most people will need to prepare the final *perfect* copy and have it reproduced in a quantity reasonable for near-term use. For the average job hunter, this would be 50 to 500 copies.

No matter which method you choose to reproduce your resume, you will need to prepare a final, error-free, fully-proofread *Master Copy* for reproduction.

You now need to select two things: the type style, also called the *typeface* or *font* you prefer. And then select the method you will use to produce your final copy.

Typefaces

Thousands of different typefaces exist throughout the world. Unless you are associated with the graphic arts or advertising industries, you may not have noticed the differences among them.

For our purposes, I will divide them into just two groups: *serif* and *sans serif* typefaces.

Each typeface, of course, usually contains both uppercase (capital) and lowercase (small) letters. *Serif* typefaces have two important features that *sans serif* typefaces do not:

- Serif typefaces also have small *appendages*, "decorative doo-dads" on the ends, tops, or bottoms of each letter.

- Serif typefaces have different *thicknesses*, as you can see in the example shown here. Each letter is both thick and thin, in different places. Here is an example of a serif typeface:

Prepared, wrote and managed distribution of
all press releases for four divisions of Mobil
in Chicago region. Supervised two part-time

- This combination of thick, then thin, makes letters that are *easier to read*, easier to scan quickly, and easier on the eyes than sans serif typefaces.

- Sans serif typefaces, which may appear to be cleaner or less cluttered, are *much* more difficult to read. The following example is identical to the one above except for the typeface.

Prepared, wrote and managed distribution of
all press releases for four divisions of Mobil
in Chicago region. Supervised two part-time

Never Mix Typefaces.

- Mixing typefaces gives your resume a cluttered appearance and makes it more difficult to read.

- Your resume will look as though you are writing a letter demanding ransom. That is *not* the effect you want to have.

Sample Typefaces

The following identical paragraphs are printed in serif and sans serif typefaces, in the easy-to-read column format. Compare for yourself and see which you prefer for readability.

Typeface Guidelines	
Possible Typeface	**Good Choice Yes/No**
Avant Garde Prepared, wrote and managed distribution of all press releases for four divisions of Mobil in Chicago region. Supervised two part-time	No Sans Serif
Helvetica Prepared, wrote and managed distribution of all press releases for four divisions of Mobil in Chicago region. Supervised two part-time	No Sans Serif
ITC Bookman Prepared, wrote and managed distribution of all press releases for four divisions of Mobil in Chicago region. Supervised two part-time	Yes Serif
Times Prepared, wrote and managed distribution of all press releases for four divisions of Mobil in Chicago region. Supervised two part-time	Yes Serif

Typeface Guidelines

Possible Typeface	Good Choice Yes/No
New Century Schoolbook Prepared, wrote and managed distribution of all press releases for four divisions of Mobil in Chicago region. Supervised two part-time	**Yes** Serif
Helvetic Condensed Prepared, wrote and managed distribution of all press releases for four divisions of Mobil in Chicago region. Supervised two part-time	**No** Sans Serif, unattractive and ordinary
Palatino Prepared, wrote and managed distribution of all press releases for four divisions of Mobil in Chicago region. Supervised two part-time	**Yes** Serif
ITC Zaph Chancery *Prepared, wrote and managed distribution of all press releases for four divisions of Mobil in Chicago region. Supervised two part-time*	**No** Serif, too gaudy, not businesslike
Times **Prepared, wrote and managed distribution of all press releases for four divisions of Mobil in Chicago region. Supervised two part-time**	**No** Serif, too heavy for resume body use, for high-lighting and headings

Make Your Resume First Class

Your final copy must be typed on a top-quality sheet of *bright white* paper. It should be a paper on which the black typeface shows up well, with good contrast between black and white.

If you use a typewriter for your final resume copy, it should be an office-quality machine, one which uses a carbon ribbon cartridge.

Old-fashioned typewriters (such as the ones many of us have in our homes) use felt or fabric ribbons. These ribbons had the advantage of lasting for months, or even years, but with each succeeding winding or use, the ribbon lost some degree of intensity. By the time you had used it several times, the contrast had diminished to poor.

Newer machines use cartridge ribbons, almost all of which are carbon ribbons or film ribbons. The older types are thick; the newer ones are thin, much like the tape in audio or video cassettes. They are wound onto the spool and then packed in cartridges, which slip easily onto your electronic typewriter or computer spindle.

Each impression made by a carbon ribbon cartridge is clean and crisp, with excellent contrast between the black letters and the white paper. Perhaps you are one of the lucky people who have access to a word processor, personal computer or a large main frame computer.

But what counts is that you must have a letter-quality printer. If it is a daisy-wheel or similar printer, it must have a carbon ribbon cartridge.

A "near letter-quality" or a dot-matrix printer is *not* acceptable.

Laser and ink-jet printers, of course, are usually excellent. Generally, laser printers also provide proportional-spacing typefaces. These allocate more space for the letter "M," for instance, than they would for the letter "I" because the "M" is much wider.

Non-proportional-spacing machines give an "I" the same amount of space as an "M," and this detracts from the readability and appearance of the words.

Resumes done according to a "formula" are sometimes frowned on by personnel professionals.

Computer Generated and Typeset Resumes

Typeset resumes have also been looked upon with skepticism by some "experts." The typeset resumes were thought to be "too slick," probably mass-produced, and possibly the work of a professional resume writer, rather than the writer's own work.

If the resume looks too much as though it was prepared according to a formula, it appears that the sender is interested in *any* job, not necessarily in the reader's specific job.

What do the experts suggest?

Have your resume on a computer diskette, or stored in your electronic typewriter.

Then print an original each time. That way, the ribbon density, type appearance, etc., will match your cover letter (individually typed at about the same time, we assume). This will create the impression that "I did this resume just for you because I'm interested in the job you have available . . . not just any job."

An added benefit, you can modify various versions easily to emphasize or de-emphasize something, to tailor the Job Objective to the position available, etc. It's more trouble for you, but it makes a much better impression than do mass-produced resumes.

Whatever method you use, do your final perfect copy on bright white paper. Then you are ready to have it reproduced in quantity. Or you can store it in memory for future additional copies.

In the fifteen years I have been reading, reviewing, and evaluating resumes, I have seen all sizes, shapes, formats, colors, typefaces, and methods of reproduction.

Even though it may seem like overkill, check the following charts to see which methods of reproduction are *acceptable*, which ones *may be acceptable*, and which are *not acceptable*, when you are making your choices.

Acceptable Means Of Reproducing Your Resume

- Offset Printing (as found at the many commercial print shops that will produce quick and economical copies for you)
- Office-quality (floor-model) photocopy machine

- Letter-quality printer with cartridge ribbon
- Computer laser printer using serif typefaces
- Office-quality electronic typewriter, serif typeface
- Office-quality electric typewriter, serif typeface

Non-acceptable Methods Of Reproducing Your Resume

- Hand-written or hand-lettered.
- Stencil process.
- Mimeograph machine.
- Fabric ribbon typewriter.
- Home-quality portable typewriter, fabric or ribbon cartridge.
- Script (simulated hand-writing) typewriter of any quality.

- Ditto process.
- All-capital-letters typewriter of any quality.
- Dot-matrix computer printer, 9-pin, 24-pin, etc.
- Near-letter-quality computer printer, any quality.
- Copy machine which produces anything less than excellent quality copies.

"Maybe" Acceptable Methods Of Reproducing Your Resume

Table-model Photocopy Machine (using plain paper)

Professional typesetting by printer or typesetter

Old-style office-quality typewriter with metal characters and featuring variable or proportional spacing

Evaluating Your Print Shop

Choose your printshop carefully. You will find considerable differences in price and quality between printers.

Ask friends for recommendations of printers. Then call or visit several to compare prices, available paper stocks, colors, weights, finishes and quality.

Ask printers to show you samples of their work. Ask if there is an extra charge for making a plate if you plan to have your resumes printed by the offset process.

If the print shop uses a photocopy machine for most resumes, make sure it makes good quality copies before your resumes are reproduced on it.

Be absolutely sure your resume is *exactly* the way you want it when you give it to the printer. It is *your* responsibility, not the printer's, if you discover a mistake after they have printed your 50, 100, or 500 resumes!

You might be surprised to learn how many people discover their mistakes *after* paying for the resume, only to have to pay *again* after the mistake has been noticed.

If the printer offers to prepare the final copy of your resume and you decide to have them do it . . . or if you turn this task over to someone other than yourself—or to someone you can watch or supervise—tell that person *not to change anything*.

Not a word. Not a space. Not a line.

Don't allow them even to move a word to another line. Not *anything*.

You are paying them, or trusting them, to *type* what you have prepared and to do so exactly as you want it done.

You are the boss. And *you* have read this book. They have not. You know more about what you want than your typist does.

You are probably right. And *they* are probably wrong.

And be sure to proofread the new version. Mistakes often creep in and you'll want to find them now before the resume is printed.

Selecting The Paper Stock For Your Resume

Color

The best color for your resume is probably a slightly off-white, eggshell shade, sometimes called ecru. The next-best color would be a classy, elegant white.

Beyond these, you might consider ivory, but not one that is too yellow. You can also use a *very* light tan or buff.

Other colors are risky. Because they may offend the reader who does not like the particular color you have selected.

What about gray? You may love it; I do. But gray, even light gray, can also look like dirty white. And black ink on dark gray, which is one of my favorite colors, is difficult to read.

All dark color papers, of course, are difficult to read. I have seen resumes printed on dark brown paper with black ink. They were difficult, almost impossible, to read.

So was a resume printed on brilliant purple, with *white-ink*. The applicant, no doubt, thought that he was going to be different. But being different is not always a positive trait. This time, it got the candidate laughed at, not admired.

Yes, a brilliant color certainly would stand out in a stack of white resumes. But just as a brilliantly-colored chartreuse home might lower property values in a neighborhood, a garish resume would almost certainly lower your value as a candidate for employment.

I know one young man who used a brilliant yellow paper, with his name boldly printed across the top in dark brown ink. It was indeed memorable.

It resembled a breakfast menu at a fast food restaurant. And normally, it would be considered in poor taste.

But he was sending it to advertising agencies—the larger ones of which receive thousands of ordinary resumes. This one stood out. And it got the candidate in.

He was granted an interview. And he got the job. (What's more, he is still there, some fifteen years later.)

But not everyone is applying to advertising agencies. So choose your color *carefully* and with an eye toward who will be reading your resume.

Texture And Weight

Paper also has *texture* differences. Linen, pebble finish, vellum, gloss, enamel, and laid finish are just a few of the many textures available.

Choose the one you like best, but consider also the person and organization you're sending it to.

For most resumes, you should select a finish which has an executive look and feel, rather than something which appeals to the emotions or to your sensual nature.

Paper also has various weights. You've noticed that some papers are very light, such as overseas airmail stationery. And that some papers are very heavy, almost like cardboard.

For the business resume, a medium weight is usually appropriate. If the printer gives you a choice between two weights, it is usually better to select the slightly heavier stock, even if it costs more.

When you receive a wedding invitation that immediately feels like a high quality paper, you get a very favorable impression even before you even open the envelope.

You should strive to create the same impression when someone first handles your resume. And you can do this by choosing your paper stock carefully.

The finest grades of paper are made of 100 percent cotton fiber, or 100 percent rag content. Most cheap papers are made of 100 percent wood pulp.

Some very fine papers are made from 75 percent wood pulp and 25 percent fiber. In the trade, printers refer to this as "25 percent rag" paper. It is quite acceptable for resumes.

Final Touches

What about colored ink?

It costs considerably more to have a special ink color for your resume. Printers normally use black ink. And every time they print in a color other than black, they must stop, clean the press completely, and change the ink—just for you.

You must pay for mixing the extra ink color especially for you, and for the time and labor required to clean and change the press. The cost for this might be as much as it costs to print your resumes in the first place.

Black ink is not only acceptable, but preferred for most business situations.

The minimum number of printed copies you should get is 100.

You may need only a few now, but the cost is slight for an extra 50 or so. Get estimates from the printer on the cost for 100 copies and for even more copies if you think you might use them.

Then opt for a number that will carry you through the next few weeks or months without having to have more printed.

Stationery And Envelopes

Stationery, which you'll need for your cover letters, can be expensive.

I recommend, in keeping with your desire to convey a good image, that you type your cover letters on good quality paper—like your resume.

Instead of going to the stationery store and paying for paper in a fancy box, ask the printer if you may purchase some stationery in bulk—the same high quality paper on which your resume is being printed.

The printer may just throw it in at no extra charge because he or she is in the printing business, not the paper business. (They buy their paper at wholesale prices.) Ask.

You may want to try to get matching business-size envelopes, too. But standard white business envelopes will do nicely in most situations.

You can buy a package of decent enough envelopes almost anywhere for a dollar or two. The printer may also have envelopes that match the paper you selected, so it is worth asking.

Some stationery stores also carry good quality writing paper in bulk, with matching envelopes. You can buy it by the pound or by the sheet. If your city is large enough to have stores that specialize in good writing papers, a phone call or two will determine which ones sell good paper in bulk (without the expensive fancy boxes and ribbons).

Now you know about good paper, the right typefaces, and the other "little things" that separate outstanding resumes from those that are merely adequate.

Taken together with the other things you have learned, you have the information to make your resume stand out for all the *right* reasons.

After more than 15 years of research and testing, I know these techniques work. Most people *strongly* prefer the resume format I have developed and now recommend to you.

Many of them are experienced executives . . . men and women who have seen thousands of resumes.

Even *they* often don't know exactly *why* they like this format. But like it, and prefer it, they do!

Chapter 6

Sample Resumes & Worksheets

Choose A Style That Fits

It's now time to actually create your resume. And you are ready to do just that.

Look over the sample resumes in the first part of this chapter. They are all based on what I have seen in *real* resumes. The names, addresses and other details have been changed, of course.

Some of the sample resumes break some of the "rules" but are included anyway. There is, after all, no "perfect" resume. Nor is there just one way to write them. Each person is different, and each resume will, likewise, have its own personality.

For each sample resume, I have written notes about the person behind the resume. This will help you to understand why that resume was done in the way it was done.

And since some of them have "flaws" of various kinds (or at least things that might have been done differently), I have added notes about these too—as well as the things I liked.

I hope this approach helps you. Look over the examples carefully and jot down ideas you want to consider for your own resume.

At the end of the chapter, after all the sample resumes, is a thorough resume worksheet. Complete it carefully and it (and the rest of the information in this book) will give you all of the information you will need to write your own resume. It is that simple.

When you are done with the worksheet use the checklist at the end of this chapter to help you avoid common resume mistakes. Pay attention to the various final tips for writing your resume to get results.

MARK M. SCOVILLE
1452 4th Avenue North
St. Cloud, Minnesota 56301
(612) 555-8201

Permanent Address:
31 Overlook Road
Blue Sky, Minnesota 55352
(612) 555-3574

Chronological resume done by college senior.
Very easy to scan and creates good image.

Job Objective: Entry Level Financial Analyst
with Portfolio Management or Financial Organization

EDUCATION

Since he is still a student, education is emphasized
by placement above the experience section.

Bachelor of Science Degree in Business Administration
St. Cloud State University, St. Cloud, Minnesota
Major: Finance, Minor: Economics
Date of Graduation: November, 1990
Grade Average: 3.146/4.0

WORK EXPERIENCE

October, 1988
to
Present

Park National Bank
St. Cloud, Minnesota

Computer Operator

Work nights; update daily files, process reports,
back-up complete computer system, print notices,
sort checks on reader sorter.

March, 1987
to
September, 1987

Able Charlie Manufacturing Corporation
Bloomington, Minnesota

Project Worker

Processed insurance claims in excess of
$1,000,000. Used Lotus 1-2-3 and dBase III
extensively.

March, 1986
to
December, 1986

Topper Automotive of Minnesota, Inc.
Goldenrod, Minnesota

Data Processing

Responsible for updating files, inventory control,
processing of reports, some data entry. Received
training at corporate office in Kansas City, Kansas.

ACTIVITIES & INTERESTS

- Selected for President's Round Table (all-university plan board)
- Vice-President, Delta Sigma Pi (business fraternity)
- President, Financial Management Association, SCSU
- Advisor, Junior Achievement; voted "Company of the Year"
- Selected and secured national speaker for Career Days
- Hobbies: sports, camping, fishing, music

Linda G. Marsala-Winston
6673 East Avenue
Lakeland, California 94544
(415) 555-1519
(415) 555-6755 (leave message)

Career Objective: Copywriter, Account Executive in
Advertising or Public Relations Agency

Experience

.   **COPYWRITER.** Developed copy for direct mail catalogues featuring collectible items, for real estate developments and for agricultural machinery and equipment.

.   **WRITER.** Wrote for Habitat magazine in London, England. Specialized on Architecture, Contemporary Lifestyles and Interior Design.

.   **SALES PROMOTION.** Fullmer's Department Store, Honolulu, Hawaii. Developed theme and copy for 1981 Grand Opening of Far East Department.

.   **FABRIC DESIGNER.** Award-winning textile designer and importer of African and South American textiles.

.   **OTHER WRITING AND PROMOTION.** News bureau chief and feature writer for college newspaper. Contributor to literary magazine. College Board Representative, Mademoiselle magazine. Scrip writer for fashion shows. Won creative writing fellowship for study in Mexico. Did public relations for International Cotton Conference. Summer graduate fellow in public information, United Nations, New York City.

.   **TEACHER.** Instructor in professional studies department of London Career Training Institute. In charge of group dynamics and career guidance modules. Organized a team for "Women in Development."

Education

.   Bachelor of Arts Degree in English, University of California, Berkeley

.   Graduate study, 30 credits completed in Journalism, University of California, Berkeley

.   Master of Arts Degree in Guidance and Counseling, California State University, Fresno

Membership

.   Member, San Francisco Women in Advertising

Jean Mary Gendlin
3939 South Fortune Circle
Reading, Pennsylvania 19600
(215) 555-0562
(215) 555-6703 (message)

Job Objective: Clerk in Retail Soft Goods or Women's Wear Store
(part-time: afternoons and weekends)

EDUCATION

Reading Wilson High School
Graduation: May, 19XX
College Preparatory Program
3.21/4.0 Grade Point Average

SCHOOL ACTIVITIES AND HONORS

. Vice-President, Future Business Leaders of America, 1990-91,
     Reading Wilson Chapter

. Selected to work as Attendance Clerk in School Office,
     junior year

. Selected to sing in Chamber Choir (one of 16 students)

. Active in girls' athletics, intramural sports activities

. Member, Home Economics Club, 2 years

EXTRACURRICULAR ORGANIZATIONS

. Secretary, church youth group; write all minutes,
          keep attendance records for funding purposes

. Honored Princess, Bethel #14, Order of Job's Daughters

WORK EXPERIENCE

. Babysitter for neighborhood families since age 11

. Summers: Counselor for girls ages 6-9,
          at YWCA Day Camp for Disabled Children, 1989, 1990

REFERENCES

. References will be furnished on request from
     employers, teachers, pastor, and others.

Brian Scott Molitor
1045 Applewood Lane
Cupertino, California 95015
(213) 422-0864
(213) 555-6642 (alternate phone)

Job Objective: Auto Mechanic

EDUCATION

San Diablo Community College
Mount Carmel, California
Certificate in Auto Mechanics; 3.25/4.0 grade average
2-year Certificate in Auto Mechanics, awarded May, 1990

Mount Carmel High School
Mount Carmel, California
Date of Graduation: June, 1988

WORK EXPERIENCE

June, 1987
to
Present

Charlie Moss Mobil Service
Mount Carmel, California

Assistant Manager/Mechanic

- Qualified in virtually all kinds of
  mechanical and electronic repairs
  on domestic and foreign cars:

  - Electronic tune-ups
  - Computer command control systems
  - Front end work and alignment
  - Transaxle work
  - Transmission diagnosis & repair
  - Complete engine overhaul

- Hired as high school student
  for summer and part-time work,
  later given responsibility to
  close & lock station, make bank
  deposits; promoted to assistant
  manager for weekend shifts.
  Supervised four employees.

June, 1986
to
May, 1987

Hunter's Pharmacy
Mount Carmel, California

Retail Sales Clerk

- Waited on customers at full-service
  pharmacy. Stocked & inventoried products.
  Made deliveries to customers. Drove van.
  Worked part-time afternoons and weekends.

SCHOOL AND COMMUNITY ACTIVITIES

- Elected Vice-president, college VICA Club, 1988-89

- Won regional and state 1st-place awards in VICA competitions, 1988, 1989 (Auto Mechanics Division)

- Active in intramural sports throughout high school

- Participated in Community Clean-up: spring, 1986 & 1987

- Played solo in annual band concert (trumpet), 1986

PERSONAL INFORMATION

Mentioning age, height, and weight are not necessary, but could be included if information will help in some way.

- Born May 13, 1966; excellent health

- Height: 5 feet, 10 inches; weight, 165 pounds

- Have overhauled four auto engines; have worked on cars as a hobby since age 13

- Other interests: all sports, fixing anything, camping

REFERENCES

"Brian is dependable and friendly. Our customers like him, and we have been pleased with his work. I would be happy if my own sons turn out like Brian."

Charlie Moss, owner
Charlie Moss Mobil Service

"Brian has been a leader in VICA and an excellent student in our Auto Mechanics program. He's not afraid of hard work, staying late, or learning new technologies. I recommend him very highly."

William Meier, Instructor
San Diablo Community College

- Additional personal and business references are available and will be furnished on request.

Andrea M. Salter
1200 Mall Avenue
State College, Pennsylvania 21101
(215) 555-6239
(215) 555-7732 (messages)

Could be done on one page, but would look too crowded and uninviting. Open format and good use of white space makes it easy to read.

CAREER OBJECTIVE:
Director of Audio Visual Instructional Media

EMPLOYMENT HISTORY

Editing could cut copy in places, allowing remainder to fit on one page, but extra details and space have value.

August, 1988
to
Present

Pennsylvania State University
State College, Pennsylvania

Head, Department of Instructional Media
Supervise 15 employees, plus 40 students as part-time staff. Propose and control budget. Administer complete department, including microforms, films, videotapes, transparencies. Provide all media services to campus:

.   graphic arts and photography
.   circulation of audio-visual equipment
.   operator assistance and scheduling
.   production of slide programs
.   production of videotapes
.   minor repairs, troubleshooting,
        and general maintenance
.   consultation on creative production
        topics to faculty & staff

Recommend and purchase hardware, software, supplies, rentals. Approve all services and procedures. Recommend and supervise design, construction and scheduling of all facilities.

Develop, implement and supervise all policies and guidelines for instructional media, including security and inventory control.

January, 1985
to
August, 1988

Kimball Broadcasting Corporation/KKBC
Las Vegas, Nevada

Assistant Engineer for Audio
Designed, updated and upgraded complete radio broadcasting facility and studio. Contracted for and supervised erecting of tower. Recommended equipment; purchased complete studio. Installed and repaired equipment.

Resume for Andrea M. Salter . Page 2

EMPLOYMENT HISTORY (continued)

Kimball Broadcasting Corporation/KKBC
Wrote operating policies and guidelines.
Insured compliance with FCC regulations.
Recommended programming policies and
changes to improve ratings. Handled all
on-location broadcasts. Worked with on-air
personalities. Trained employees.

EDUCATION

Master of Science Degree in Media, 1985
University of Wisconsin - Stout
Grade average: 3.85/4.0

Bachelor of Arts Degree in Business Administration
University of Southern Iowa, 1983
Rolland, Iowa

PROFESSIONAL AFFILIATIONS

Information gives impression job seeker gets involved and will succeed in her profession.

. Listed in "Who's Who in American Colleges
and Universities," 1982-1983

. Instructor in Media Techniques, University of Southern Iowa

. Member, Business and Professional Media People

REFERENCES

. Business, personal and educational references
are available and will be furnished on request

Conor R. O'Brien
14567 Treeful Lane
Walnut Springs, New Jersey 01111
(202) 555-6421
(202) 555-6602 (leave message)

Successfully used combination resume to escape disagreeable boss and get into sales side of computer industry. Background in field service and management are strong points for selling systems into similar environments.

OBJECTIVE: to be a hands-on, accomplished **MANAGER**
selling and providing high-quality technical services
in the computer hardware or software industry

SUMMARY OF EXPERIENCES   This summary is extra, not necessary, but is nice touch.

- Plant Manager: 100%-responsible for production of state-of-the-art
  advanced electronics equipment
- Planner and Achiever: Analyzing situations to achieve specific goals and results
- Financial Manager: Manage complex projects with budgetary concerns in mind

ACHIEVEMENTS

- Promoted to Leading Support Technician in charge of
  Englander Electronics' Rohrer System
- Successfully dealt with customers, salesmen and
  field service technicians using honesty, diplomacy
  and confidence; provided superior technical support
- Personally evaluated and selected all test equipment used in
  manufacturing end-product (over $100,000 worth of equipment)
- Directly responsible for expanding and maintaining manufacturing
  workforce that grew over 500% in 3 years (began with one person,
  grew to 20 people)

EXPERIENCE

Deather Instrument Company, Earthworm, New Jersey
Production Manager 1986 to present
Manufacturer of state-of-the-art electrocardiograph equipment

- Responsible for overseeing manufacturing
  of medical electronics from prototype to
  finished product (1988 sales: $10,000,000)

Englander Electronics,   Mollica, New Jersey
Field Service Engineer   1981 to 1986
Manufacturer of electrocardiographs and intensive care monitors

- Hired as production technician; promoted
  through system to Tech Support Engineer
  to top position as **Field Service Engineer**

Buzzell Controls Manufacturing Company, Loveland, New Jersey
Manufacturing Consultant   1979 to 1981
Manufacturer of high grade industrial motor controls

Resume could be forced into one page format, but would look crowded and not be as effective.

PERSONAL INFORMATION

. Honor Student in college; selected for Director's Honors List

. Member, Electronics Club, 1977-78, 1978-79

. Earned 100% of college expenses by working in retail sales at Spring Garden Center (3 years)

. Enjoy playing basketball, scuba diving, swimming, all sports

. Played church league basketball, 2 years; played in 2 summer softball leagues

. Have traveled throughout entire United States, Alaska, Hawaii, on business and for pleasure

. Hobbies: photography, woodworking, home ownership

. Happily married to Lisa O'Brien since 1982; 2 children, ages 3 and 2

EDUCATION

Waltrip County Technical College
Associate Degree in Electronics, 1979

Amy Ann Towson
4848 Sedler Parkway
Billings, Montana 59101
(406) 555-7856

CAREER OBJECTIVE: Secretarial Position in Broadcasting
Requiring Excellent Word Processing Skills and Some Public Contact

EDUCATION

Secretarial Office Skills Institute
Seattle, Washington
Diploma in Secretarial Science
Graduation: June, 1991
Honor Student; 3.5 overall grade average

East High School
Billings, Montana
Graduation: May, 1988
"B+" grade average; elected to Honor Roll

WORK EXPERIENCE

September, 1988
to
Present

Bruce, Carl & Douglas Law Offices
Seattle, Washington

Office Assistant
Typed correspondence, reports, simple briefs,
and various forms for attorneys and paralegals.
Answered phone, took messages, and acted
as fill-in receptionist. Part-time job while
attending Secretarial Office Skills Institute.

Skill levels: type 70 words per minute,
take shorthand at normal conversational speed,
operate IBM-compatible personal computer
and all normal office equipment (calculator,
photocopier, postage meter, mail room machines).

September, 1985
to
May, 1988

East High School
Billings, Montana

Office Assistant
Typed reports and forms, ran errands,
processed attendance reports, and answered
phone; part-time job during free periods,
after school and on some vacation days.

<u>Amy Ann Towson</u>   .   <u>Page 2</u>

<u>WORK EXPERIENCE</u> (continued)

Summers, 1987,   <u>All-Hours Convenience Store</u>
1988, 1989   Billings, Montana

                                  <u>Clerk</u>
                                  Sold packaged products, deli items, sandwiches;
                                  stocked shelves; took inventory; acted as
                                  Assistant Manager during absence of regular
                                  managers (given key to store, made bank
                                  deposits).

Summers, 1987,   <u>Family Nursing Home</u>
1988, 1989   Billings, Montana

                                  <u>Volunteer Aide</u>
                                  Assisted staff with projects; visited with residents;
                                  helped in crafts sessions and sing-alongs. Worked
                                  4-6 hours weekly.

CIVIC AND COMMUNITY ACTIVITIES   Includes number of points in this section. Details could give an edge.

        .   Volunteered for "Habitat for Humanity" project;
                 met and worked with ex-President Carter.

         .   Active on Academy Student Council; helped plan
                 school picnic, field trips, and other student events.

        .   Secretary, East High School Office Careers Club;
                 elected by classmates.

        .   Active in church youth group; elected to
                 various offices, including President.

Daniel A. Kohl
3606 Roxboro Road
Atlanta, Georgia 30326-1455
(404) 551-4040

JOB OBJECTIVE: Systems Analyst / Management Information Systems

WORK EXPERIENCE
ACCOMPLISHMENTS

- Exceeded 135% of sales quota, won "leading salesperson award" calling exclusively on new prospects to sell point-of-purchase recordkeeping and cash flow systems for Sweda Division, Litton Industries

- Qualified programmer, trainer, installer for data processing equipment. Achieved 50% of sales through referral of clients. "Dan was the best sales and service representative we've ever had calling on us," said Allan Koehn, CEO, Circle G. Restaurants.

- Developed complete recordkeeping and accounting system for Georgia's largest cosmetics wholesaler. Trained employees, supervised initial operations, de-bugged system.

- Increased sales 71% over prior year in Georgia/Florida territory for Chicago-based manufacturer of electric blankets and appliances (Midwest Appliances Corporation).

EDUCATION

- Graduated from University of Illinois, 1977, Marketing/Management major, Bachelor of Science Degree

- Currently enrolled in graduate studies, Georgia State University, Atlanta, leading to MBA degree with computer science emphasis

- Graduated from Harcourt College, private business college. Awarded 2-year Associate Degree in Business

- Graduated from NCR School, Computer Programming, 1978

Resume of Daniel Kohl . Page 2

PERSONAL INFORMATION

- President, college fraternity, Tau Sigma Epsilon

- New editor, University of Illinois Campus Events newspaper

- Enjoy sports, classical music, reading business books

- Member, Buckhead Jaycees; chair, Special Olympics Project (raised $8,000 for fund)

EMPLOYMENT HISTORY

Record of holding jobs not good because of moving around. It is tucked on second page. Could have used skills resume to hide tenure on jobs completely.

- November, 1980 to Present: Territory Sales Representative Sweda Division, Litton Industries Atlanta, Georgia

- November, 1978 to November, 1980: Sales Representative Collins Cosmetics Corporation Atlanta, Georgia

- November, 1977 to October, 1978: District Sales Manager Midwest Appliances Corp., Chicago

- Held various part-time sales jobs during college years to support myself independently; paid all college tuition and expenses

PERSONAL INFORMATION

- Willing to travel if desired; have traveled widely throughout United States, Canada, Mexico

Norman P. Mindell
1042 North Amber Way
Charlotte, North Carolina
(602) 555-8745 (work)
(602) 555-9631 (answering service)

<u>**JOB OBJECTIVE:**</u>
<u>**Automobile Dealership New Car Sales Manager**</u>

<u>WORK EXPERIENCE</u>

October, 1986
to
Present

<u>Sanders Chevrolet</u>
Charlotte, North Carolina

<u>Used Car Sales Manager</u>

Sell used cars and manage sales force
of four salespeople. Consistently exceed
quota by at least 10%, often 25%.
Have own clientele; 30% of personal production
is from referrals and recommendations.
Conduct sales meetings for staff.
Hold training sessions; establish
sales quotas for dealership. Purchase
cars at auctions; travel to various auctions.
Awarded trip to Hawaii for performance.

April, 1984
to
October, 1986

<u>Sanders Chevrolet</u>
Charlotte, North Carolina

<u>Sales Representative, Used Cars</u>

Sold used cars. Consistently averaged sales
of 25 cars monthly in good months, 15 cars
in slow months. Set company record for
unit sales and total volume. Promoted
to Sales Manager after 2 and 1/2 years over
salespeople with more experience and
seniority. Started as part-timer while
attending college full-time.

<u>PERSONAL INFORMATION</u>

. <u>Graduated</u> from Piedmont Junior College
Associate Degree in Marketing, Class of 1984

. <u>Honor Roll Student:</u> 3.47 grade average;
Vice President of Marketing Club

. Have <u>enjoyed cars as a hobby</u> since childhood.
Mechanically inclined; built kit car at age 20.

. <u>Active in church and civic affairs</u>. Member, Jaycees.
Host and referee/judge, Special Olympics.

Amy Jo Gibbs
Apartment #206
32 Towne Circle
Philadelphia, Pennsylvania 19177
(215) 555-3911
(215) 555-7675 (for messages)

> Good example of one page resume with good use of white space, underlining and bold type. Attractive.

Career & Job Target: Assistant Buyer for Fashion or Soft Goods

EDUCATION

> Resume puts education up top for recent graduate. Is more important than for person with significant work experience.

Fashion Academy of Philadelphia
Associate Degree in Fashion Merchandising
Graduated "With Honors," June, 1990

Toledo Area Community College, Toledo, Ohio
Studied Business and Conversational French

Woodrow Wilson High School, Toledo, Ohio
Graduated May, 1987; B+ average, upper 1/4 of class

WORK EXPERIENCE

> Left out dates of employment. For older worker, many employers would suspect resume is hiding job gaps or other problems. For a young worker, with little paid work experience, it does no harm.

- Retail Sales Representative, "The Up Shop"
  Warrington's Department Store, Philadelphia

  Sell business clothing and ensembles for business women in special section of store. Assisted in some buying decisions. Worked 30 hours per week while attending Fashion Academy of Philadelphia. Assigned to supervise training program for two high school co-op students.

- Sales Clerk in Cosmetics, Walgreen's
  Toledo, Ohio (two years)

  Sold cosmetics at counter part-time while in high school. Received school credit under school's Marketing Education co-op program.

COMMUNITY AND SCHOOL ACTIVITIES & ORGANIZATIONS

> Are all school related but helps indicate energy and leadership potential.

- Vice President, Fashionettes Modeling Club
  (sponsors of annual charity "Fashion Fair" to raise scholarship funds for students and charitable causes)

- Member, Student Senate, Fashion Academy, 2 years

- High school: marching band, sports, various clubs, Honor Roll

John M. Thomas
2248 North 67th Avenue
Phoenix, Arizona 85355
(602) 555-5623 (Home)
(602) 555-1428 (Message)

JOB OBJECTIVE: Advertising Art Director
(Layout, Design, Illustration) . . . in a position
using my communication abilities in working well with others

EXPERIENCE

October, 1983
to
June, 1990

Turnbull, Teller and Witsend Advertising
Phoenix, Arizona

Art Director

- Work with account executives, copywriters, creative director to create and develop initial ideas for clients, often under tight deadlines. Supervise five artists; delegate assignments, work with printers, paper suppliers, typographers.

- Work on Macintosh II Desktop Publisher using Adobe, PageMaker, Lightspeed and other software programs.

- Accounts include:
  - Union Batteries . Abbott Seeds
  - Color Factory . Suburban Pools
  - Motel 8 . Hartwell Home Organs
  - Area Chevy Dealers . Med Pharm
  - 1st National Bank . Romer Faucets
  - KinderCare Institute . MillWay Homes

February, 1977
to
October, 1983

Roberson and Michaels Advertising
Scottsdale, Arizona

Art Director

- Layout, keyline/paste-up for local, regional, and national accounts: motels, drycleaners, hobby shops, auto dealers, shopping malls, national Foodsaver markets chain.

June, 1975
to
February, 1977

Sun Valley Banking Corporation
Phoenix, Arizona

Artist & Designer

- Prepared in-house ads, brochures, mailers, inserts, annual reports, forms.

Resume of John Thomas . Page 2

SPECIAL PROJECTS

- Won National First Place Award for Phoenix Junior Advertising Club as chair of competitive creative team for Y-Pals (YMCA program for fatherless boys), 1982.

- Freelance illustration and design for Hewlett-Packard, Sky Harbor Airport, Arizona Medical Society, McDonald's.

EDUCATION

- Arizona State University Bachelor of Fine Arts Degree in Visual Communications
- Degree granted June, 1975

- Valley High School Phoenix, Arizona Graduated with diploma, honors

HOBBIES & INTERESTS

- Photography, illustration, outdoor sports, family events with wife, Andrea, and three children

David C. German
1604 North 105th Street
Nashville, Tennessee 37200
(615) 555-0789 (leave message)

Career Objective:
Teaching Position in Junior High or Middle School
in Social Studies, Geography or Government

EDUCATION
Tennessee College, Nashville, Tennessee
Bachelor of Arts, May, 1991
Major: Education   Minor: Social Studies & Geography
Grade Average: 3.7 on 4.0 System

Johnson City High School, Johnson City, Tennessee
Graduated June, 1987
Ranked 28th in class of 415

HONORS, AWARDS AND ACHIEVEMENTS

- Dean's List, Tennessee College (3.5 required)

- Selected for listing and membership (junior year) in "Who's Who in American Colleges and Universities"

- Winner, Scroll Award for Academic and Service Leadership

- President, Kappa Delta Pi, National Education Honor Society, (Tennessee College Chapter)

- Treasurer, Phi Eta Sigma, National Freshman Honor Society (Tennessee College Chapter)

- Co-Chair, Campus Chest, 1989 and 1990; raised $6,000 for Emergency Student Loan Fund

- Selected for membership, Tennessee College Activities Board, junior and senior years

- Selected for Winterim Social Planning Board

- High School: elected to National Honor Society in junior year; member and officer of numerous clubs and organizations; teacher's aide (for kindergarten) for one semester

WORK EXPERIENCE

- September, 1990 to May, 1991
Tennessee College, Nashville, Tennessee
Activities Program Facilitator

Planned programming for residence hall activities.
Liaison between Resident Assistants and Administration.
Published residence hall newsletter. Gained experience
in advising, counseling and referral of students for
professional counseling.

Resume of **David C. German** . Page 2

WORK EXPERIENCE (continued)
.   September, 1989 to December, 1990
           Tennessee College
           Geography Lab Assistant

      .   Aided students in audio-visual tutorial laboratory.

      .   September, 1988 to May, 1989
           Tennessee College
           Dormitory Switchboard Operator

      .   Summers, 1987 through 1990
           Summer painting and maintenance for various employers
           in Johnson City, Tennessee (names furnished on request)

PERSONAL INFORMATION   Has selected information that supports job objective and image as energetic and well rounded.

      .   President, United Christian Youth Organizations
           (consortium of all Johnson City church youth groups);
           active member, church youth group; president, senior year

      .   Play piano, string bass, guitar

      .   Enjoy athletics and all sports, growing plants, travel

      .   Earned 80% of college expenses through scholarships
           and personal earnings

KAREN E. MULLIGAN

669 Dart Drive
Marietta, Georgia 30033
(404) 555-1571
(404) 555-4534 (alternate phone)

EDUCATION

Emory University School of Law
Atlanta, Georgia
Class of 19XX

University of Alabama, Huntsville
Graduated February, 1988, with high honors: "Magna Cum Laude"
Bachelor of Arts degree; Major, psychology; minor, political science

Decatur High School, Decatur, Alabama
Class of 1983

HONORS, AWARDS AND ACHIEVEMENTS

- Selected "Outstanding Graduate," Department of Psychology, University of Alabama, Huntsville, 1988

- Elected to Pi Sigma Alpha, political science honor society

- Elected to Alpha Lambda Delta, freshman honor society

- Selected for all-university Concert Committee; worked for four years to help select concerts for campus and community

- Elected to Senior and Junior Honor Societies, high school

- Won varsity tennis letter, 2 years; basketball letter, 2 years

WORK EXPERIENCE

- **Cabaret Director,** University of Alabama, Huntsville
  September, 1986 to February, 1988

  Scheduled bands, comedians and other talent acts for university performances. Negotiated contracts, prices, arrangements; handled details for university; supervised productions; hosted artists and performers. Attended regional and national Student Activities conventions.

- **Self-employed Leather-crafter,** 1981 through 1988

  Filled custom orders for leather goods (wholesale and retail). Sold several large orders to local specialty shops.

- **Bartender,** T.G.I. Friday's, Huntsville, Alabama, 1987-1989

  Earned college tuition and expense money with part-time work; later promoted to full-time status.

Stephen H. Zigman   .   1458 Rockford Avenue South   .   Springfield, Maine 11342
(207) 555-7845   .   Alternate phone: (207) 555-9613 for messages

One page combination resume highlights what was done rather than where he worked. Emphasizes accomplishments over job titles and dates of employment. Approach works to his benefit because it allows him to present strengths.

Job Objective: Manufacturer's Representative for Audio-Stereo Products

Uses summary to present overview of abilities. Can be quite effective.

Summary: Set all-new store sales records at Springfield's leading audio equipment retailer for 1986-1990. Sold $1,000,000+ in audio lines. Promoted to manager in June, 1990.

Use of "bullets" can call attention to items in a list.

Accomplishments:

. Won Fisher regional sales award, 1988, for being top salesperson in state

. Awarded trip to Chicago for Consumer Electronics Show, June, 1988, by JBL for excellence in speaker sales in 1987

. Developed sales lead-and-follow-up system used by store for improving sales; store sales increased 44% over prior year

. Graduated with honors from marketing program, Ogunquit Community College, 1985

. Soldier of the Month, Fort Sumter, May, 1982

. Active church member, usher, on committees for several church-related groups

. Was Big Brother to young man for three years, 1987-1989, for Big Brothers of America

. Member, Toastmasters Clubs of America, local chapter; winner of several local awards for public speaking

Short descriptions of work history details give employers helpful information. Use this unless there are job gaps or other problems.

Employment History:

February, 1986, to Present:
Audio Perfection, 2000 Main Street, Springfield, Maine

June, 1983, to February, 1986:
Zigman Contractors, 3652 Third Street, Springfield, Maine (father's company; worked as laborer, helper, carpenter)

June, 1980, to June, 1983:
U. S. Army, radio communications specialist

Education section on bottom due to significant Work experience.

Education:

. Ogunquit Community College. 1983-1985
Graduated with Associate Degree in Business Administration

. Springfield High School
Graduated in upper 1/3 of class, June, 1980

David W. Browne
1546 Lindwall Terrace
Northbrook, Illinois 60062
(312) 555-6144 (home)
(312) 555-0004 (office)

BACKGROUND SUMMARY

Fifteen years of management-level experience in materials planning, manufacturing, warehousing, distribution, traffic and facilities planning

EMPLOYMENT HISTORY

1987
to
Present

Midwest Medicalhelp Company
Northbrook, Illinois

Corporate Distribution and Traffic Manager

. Administer 4 regional warehouses in $40-million (annual sales) medical firm.
. Negotiate all carrier rates and insure publication of appropriate tariffs.
. Established national delivery network for home delivery to dialysis patients. Lowered rate costs by 10%, resulting in savings of $80,000 annually.
. Reduced transportation costs by 13%, for savings of $25,000 per year.
. Lowered expenses for outside warehouses by 42% by closing undesirable locations; selected site for new warehouse.
. Responsible for all international imports and exports.

1973
to
1987

1984 to 1987

Worldwide Medical Products Corporation
Deerfield, Illinois

Operations Manager

. Created, developed and installed new conveyor system; increased operational efficiency of outbound orders by 30%. Resulted in cost savings of $75,000 per year.
. Planned and implemented office and warehouse layouts for both expanding and new facilities.
. Prepared budget of $1.6 million for 30 pharmacy branches in USA. Control all capital spending for same 30 locations.
. Created new computer program to track performance of all branches on percentage of orders filled.
. Developed computer program to monitor cost-per-order at all locations for 30,000 orders monthly.

Resume of **David Browne** . Page 2

<u>1981 to 1984</u>	**Planning Manager**

.   Designed and opened new Home Patient
Distribution Centers. Chose inventory,
trained all personnel. All projects completed
on time and within budgets.
.   Developed, wrote and published turnkey
Startup Manual for opening all new branches.

<u>1978 to 1981</u>   **Patient Service Operations Manager**

.   Opened and managed company's first
Home Care facility. Supervised 12 employees.
.   Recommended and installed new inventory
system to process 50% order-volume increase
with no increase in number of employees.
.   Designed and opened company's next three
Home Care facilities. Wrote and published first
Policy and Procedures Manual.

<u>1973 to 1978</u>   **Training Manager; Int'l. Distribution Manager;
On-Site Plant Production Analyst; Inventory Analyst**

1972
to
1973

Banner Home Systems
Muncie, Indiana

Material Control Foreman

EDUCATION AND TRAINING

> Education supports current job objective. Has included additional related training. Due to these experiences, education is listed at bottom.

.   Bachelor of Science Degree in Business Administration
Ball State University, Muncie, Indiana; June, 1968
.   Certificates: "Quality Control & Zero Defects"
Crosby Quality College;
"Problem Solving"
Kepner-Tregoe Management Institute

PERSONAL INFORMATION

> Details including physical fitness, activity in church, and a happy marriage can impress employer, but are not essential.

.   Married, 2 children; excellent health; willing to travel
.   Hobbies: running, all sports, home repair projects
.   Elected to Church Council, 800-member congregation
.   Member, Council of Logistics Management;
Member, Warehouse Education and Research Council

Virginia Haskell Gordon
4467A 19th Avenue South
Des Moines, Iowa 50301
(219) 555-6639 (home)
(219) 555-4868 (leave message)

Job Objective: Legal Assistant

EDUCATION

Des Moines Community College, Des Moines, Iowa
Diploma in Paralegal Studies
Graduated with honors in June, 1990

Storm Lake High School, Storm Lake, Iowa
Graduated May, 1968
B+ average; ranked in upper 20% of class

EXPERIENCE

March, 1987
to
August, 1990

Blue Line Temporary Services
Des Moines, Iowa

Temporary-help assignments included:

Legal Secretary:
Worked in eleven law offices, ranging
in size from 1 to 47 attorneys. Performed
all office duties: type 75 wpm, shorthand,
operate legal software and word processing
equipment, answer phone, act as
receptionist. Familiar with briefs,
legal terminology, court documents,
correspondent firms, transcripts, etc.

Radio Traffic Clerk
Scheduled commercial radio spots
for air time. Took instruction from
advertising agencies and program
director. Acted as liaison with on-air
personalities.

Secretary to Sales Manager
Took minutes and notes at all sales
meetings. Typed all correspondence,
including confidential business material.
Acted as hostess & conducted office tours
for visiting executives and clients.

Virginia Haskell Gordon . Page 2

WORK EXPERIENCE (continued) Large unemployment gap not explained. Most employers will assume time off for raising a family.

June, 1968 to October, 1983	**Meils Ford-Lincoln-Mercury** Storm Lake, Iowa **Secretary-Receptionist / Office Manager** Performed all secretarial and office duties for small-town auto dealership. Typed letters, completed weekly and monthly reports. Answered phones. Handled some sales inquiries. Worked with accountant to complete all financial statements and reports. Did billing and bookkeeping.

PERSONAL INFORMATION Entries show productivity during time not employed in wage paying job.

- Married, 3 grown children

- Elected vice-president, Paralegal Club (college); arranged for speakers; planned Chicago trip

- Active in church and school activities; past president, Wilson School PTA

- Enjoy skiing, flower arranging, reading, current events discussion groups

- Volunteer, Breadbasket Food Pantry for homeless

Amanda Perez
N43 W2716 Highway G
Curran, Illinois 60542
(813) 555-3242 (residence)
(813) 555-3555 (answering service)

Job Objective: Sales Representative for
Pharmaceutical Manufacturer/Distributor

WORK EXPERIENCE

MARKETING

.   Managed $350,000 marketing campaign for church fund drive. Achieved 12% increase in gifts/pledges.

.   Organized volunteer sales force; used demographic data to assign sales teams.

.   Wrote series of sales letters. Conducted planning meetings, set target dates, delegated follow-up responsibilities. Assisted in training teams on scripts, presentations, "asking for the order."

.   Organized new volunteer program for community hospital: gift shop, front desk, readers, sitters, etc. Recruited and maintained initial volunteer corps at 32 people; added 30 people in next twelve months.

EMPLOYMENT HISTORY

.   1975-Present: Registered Nurse, Cole County Hospital Cardiac Care and Intensive Care Units.

.   1971-1975: Medical Assistant, Stephen Brey, M.D. Assisted with routine medical tasks supervised by registered nurse and physician.

EDUCATION

.   Bachelor of Science Degree in Nursing
Missouri Western University
Degree awarded June, 1975; GPA 3.42/4.0

.   Medical Assistant Certificate
Cole County Community College
Graduated May, 1972; GPA 3.75/4.0

.   George Carson High School, diploma, 1970
Fortuna, Missouri

PERSONAL INFORMATION

.   Drive own car; willing to travel overnight; excellent health

.   Received $500 annual scholarship from Women's League for five years ($2500 total) for post-high-school education

Jennifer Lynn Olson
4842 Lombard Court
Chicago, Illinois 60608
(312) 555-6864
(312) 555-7753 (leave message)

> Bold type used for section heads and underlining of important information. Helps reader scan for essential information avoiding cluttered look.

Job Objective: Beautician/Cosmetologist

EDUCATION

International Beauty Academy
406 North Wabash Avenue
Chicago, Illinois 60606
Graduated from 1-year course in June, 1990

Wilbur Wright College, Chicago
Completed one-year of liberal arts studies

Northside High School, Chicago
Graduated in June, 1988

WORK EXPERIENCE

> Due to little formal work experience, included training and other information to be considered.

- Completed six-week internship in cosmetology at North-Clark Beauty Studios, Chicago, Illinois Received all "excellent" ratings and evaluations from beauticians and supervisors. Spring, 1990.

- Supermarket Checker at Smartway Food Market, 3650 North Clark Street, Chicago. Earned all tuition and expenses for college and beauty school plus money for rent, clothes, personal items. Received commendations from Store Manager for good performance and for receiving customer compliments. September, 1987 to Present.

- Babysitter for neighborhood families. Supervised and cared for children 2-8 years old. Also did some house cleaning duties for these families as needed.

COMMUNITY AND SCHOOL ACTIVITIES

> Section also presents non-work experience showing ability to handle a variey of responsibilities. When work experience increases, much of this section can be cut.

- Member, Northside Swing Choir, all three years. Sang in all concerts, participated in choir trips.

- Member, Future Business Leaders of America

- Lab Assistant, Typing Class

- Participated in intramural sports

- Elected secretary, church youth group, senior year. Active member of group throughout high school.

Kevin Wong
4350 Highland Avenue
Tucson, Arizona 85772
(602) 555-7876
(602) 555-2232 (message service)

Job Objective: Electronics Technician

EDUCATION

Arizona Electronics & Technical Institute
Phoenix, Arizona
Associate Degree in Electronics Technology
Grade point average: 3.56 on 4.0 scale
Graduated June, 1991; courses included:

. Digital Electronics	. AF & RF Analog Electronics
. Microprocessors	. Fabrication
. Circuit Design	. Design Applications
. Hands-on Repair	. Communications

Tucson North High School
Honors Grades in Math, Science and Drawing
Received diploma in May, 1989

WORK EXPERIENCE

. Unified Telephone Company
Tucson, Arizona

Responsible for troubleshooting and repairing
various types of telephones, including cordless,
dial, touchtone, and full-feature desk phones.

Worked from September, 1989 to Present.

. Bob's Big Boy Restaurant
Tucson, Arizona

Busboy, Waiter. Commended as "one of my best
workers" by restaurant manager.

Worked two years, part-time after school.

SCHOOL AND COMMUNITY ACTIVITIES

. Member, Math Club, Kit Car Club, Letterman's Club

. Assistant coach for Cub Scout Baseball Team

Ronald P. Andrews
1437 Richer Avenue
East Town, Maryland 21602
(805) 555-8943
Leave messages: 555-6562

Job Objective: Computer Repair Technician

EDUCATION

International Computer Institute
Washington, D.C.
Diploma in Computer Repair, June, 1990
Completed 18-month training program; "B" average

Walter Raleigh High School
East Town, Maryland
Graduated in June, 1987

WORK HISTORY

September, 1988
to
Present

ArData Computer Systems: "The Computer Store"
Washington, D.C.

Troubleshoot and repair IBM-compatible MS-DOS
computer systems, including hard disk drives; dot matrix,
inkjet and laser printers; laptop portables and desktop models.

Familiar with various brands of equipment; able to diagnose
simple or complex malfunctions. Read schematic diagrams.
Enjoy mechanical as well as electronic work. Worked part-time
to earn tuition and expense money for computer school.

June, 1986
to
September, 1988

CopyQuick Instant Printers
East Town, Maryland

Counter clerk and printer at instant print shop.
Waited on customers. Advised on paper, ink, quantities,
paper selection, binding. Ran printing equipment for
hundreds of different types of print jobs, including
multi-color work. Worked after school and weekends
as needed.

MEMBERSHIPS, CLUBS AND ACTIVITIES

- Varsity baseball team, Letterman's Club officer

- Member, Electronics Club, Ham Radio Club

- Volunteer Camp Counselor, summer church camp

Jerry P. Longarrow
2961 Passmore Circle
Tulsa, Oklahoma 74196
(303) 555-2349

Job Objective: Retail Men's Clothing Salesperson

EDUCATION
Maxwell High School
Maxwell, Kansas
"B" Average; upper 40% of class
Graduated June, 1991

- Received A's and B's in Marketing Education Classes

- Took college preparatory subjects: algebra, English, sociology, psychology, plus business subjects: accounting, economics, business law, marketing and salesmanship.

- Won regional and state prizes in marketing competitions, 1991

WORK EXPERIENCE

- September, 1989 to Present

Edgar's Men's Wear
Maxwell, Kansas

Salesman for Men's Wear Store

Worked after school and weekends in full-line men's wear retail store in city of 35,000. Sold suits, sport coats, shirts, ties, and all related types of clothing and accessories. Average sales of $1,000 per 40-hour week. Developed own customers. Eligible for re-hire.

After first year, Mr. William Edgar also asked me to work full-time in summer. "You've done excellent work, Jerry, and we want you with us full time."

PERSONAL INFORMATION

- Currently attending Tulsa Junior College studying marketing and business

- Excellent health; active in sports and fitness

- Member, Maxwell Drum & Bugle Band (trumpet)

- Business and personal references are available and will be furnished on request

Resume Worksheet

Instructions. Complete each section as you want this information to appear on your resume itself. Be complete. Do not use abbreviations unless necessary. Be brief. Emphasize your accomplishments and skills that are directly related to the job you want. And use a pencil to allow you to make changes later.

Many people find it helpful to write out a draft version of the more complicated sections on other sheets of paper first. *Then* go ahead and complete this worksheet. Use additional pages as needed so that what you write on the worksheet here is very close to what you want to put on your resume.

IDENTIFICATION

Full Name: _____

Address: _____

City: _____

State or Province: _____

ZIP or Postal Code: _____

Phone Numbers. List these as they will appear on your resume. Include your area code within the parentheses. The optional comment lines are for brief comments such as "home #," "office #" "leave message" or whatever.

Primary Phone Number: (_____) _____ - _____

Comment: _____

Alternate Phone Number: (_____) _____ - _____

Comment: _____

EDUCATION & TRAINING

Begin with your most recent education or training. If you have attended many schools, condense these into a manageable number. Look for the best way to display your educational experiences; usually, that will be a listing of the *one or two* schools where you did the work which led directly into the career you are in. Or the programs where you received your most important, or most impressive-sounding training.

(Give the month and year you graduated, or the class in which you were enrolled, such as "Class of 1989;" "June, 1988;" "Graduation: December, 1990;" etc.)

SCHOOL NAME: _____

City, State or Province: _____

Class: _____

List degree, certificate or diploma received: _____

Major: _____

Minor(s): _____

Overall grade point average or class standing: _____

Grade point average in subjects related to job: _____

Resume Worksheet

EDUCATION & TRAINING (continued)

Related activities and accomplishments: _____

_____

_____

_____

_____

SCHOOL NAME: _____

City, State or Province:_____

Class: _____

List degree, certificate or diploma received: _____

_____

Major:_____

Minor(s): _____

Overall grade point average or class standing:_____

Grade point average in subjects related to job: _____

Related activities and accomplishments: _____

_____

_____

_____

_____

SCHOOL NAME: _____

City, State or Province:_____

Class: _____

List degree, certificate or diploma received: _____

_____

Major:_____

Minor(s): _____

Overall grade point average or class standing:_____

Grade point average in subjects related to job: _____

Related activities and accomplishments: _____

_____

_____

_____

_____

Resume Worksheet

WORK EXPERIENCE

Begin with your most recent full-time work experiences and work back in time. Devote more space to recent jobs or jobs that are more relevant to support the job you want now.

CURRENT OR MOST RECENT JOB

Name of Organization: _____

City, State or Province: _____

Date you started working there: _____

(Month and Year only, name of month spelled out)

Date you ended your employment there: _____

(Resumes often state "Present," as in "June, 1986 to Present," even though you no longer are working there. This is not considered untruthful by most, but you can also list the month you left. It is no longer considered unusual to be unemployed and seeking employment for several months; it's normal.)

Job Title: _____

_____

(If you held several job titles at one organization, please see the resume examples for several good ideas to easily make this situation understandable.)

Job Description. Tell what you did, as clearly and exactly as you can. Emphasize *results* and *accomplishments* directly attributable to the fact that you were there. Whenever possible, use numbers, percentages, increases, dollar figures to indicate some *exactness* in what you accomplished while there.

_____

_____

_____

_____

_____

_____

_____

NEXT JOB

Name of Organization: _____

City, State or Province: _____

Date you started working: _____

Date you ended your employment: _____

Job Title: _____

_____

(If you held several job titles at one organization, please see the resume examples for several good ideas to easily make this situation understandable.)

Resume Worksheet

WORK EXPERIENCE (continued)

Job Description. Unless this job is important in supporting your current job objective, be briefer with its description. Eliminate repetitions. List only important results and accomplishments, duties or responsibilities.

_____

_____

_____

_____

_____

_____

_____

NEXT JOB

Name of Organization: _____

City, State or Province: _____

Date you started working: _____

Date you ended your employment: _____

Job Title: _____

_____

Job Description. Unless this job is important in supporting your current job objective, be even briefer here. If you can hold it down to a few phrases, even to two phrases or three, that would be fine. Try it.

_____

_____

_____

_____

_____

_____

_____

NEXT JOB

Name of Organization: _____

City, State or Province: _____

Date you started working: _____

Date you ended your employment: _____

Job Title: _____

_____

Resume Worksheet

WORK EXPERIENCE (continued)

Job Description. If you have more than four previous jobs, consider simple listings here—or combine all of those "miscellaneous" jobs into one statement like "held various positions while going to school."

_____

_____

_____

_____

_____

_____

HONORS, AWARDS AND ACHIEVEMENTS

What non-school-related organizations did you join? Church group? 4-H? Job's Daughters? Key Club? Volunteers? ROTC? Political campaigns? Musical groups? Non-school sports? Coaching? Tutoring?

Name of Organization: _____

My Role:_____

_____

_____

_____

_____

_____

_____

_____

PERSONAL INFORMATION

Include any special skills, attributes, hobbies or other information that support your job objective but that don't fit elsewhere.

_____

_____

_____

_____

_____

_____

Resume Worksheet

PERSONAL INFORMATION

WHAT OTHERS SAY

If you choose to include testimonials in your resume, put the statements you want to include here.

_____

_____

_____

_____

_____

_____

_____

_____

_____

_____

_____

_____

_____

_____

_____

_____

References

You do not need to include references on your resume. If space permits, you can add an optional statement such as:

> *Business and personal references are available and will be furnished on request.* or

> *Excellent business and personal references are available.* or

> *Complete business and personal references are available and will gladly be furnished on request.*

Congratulations! Now you are ready to put together your resume's final draft. Before you begin, take a look at the *common resume mistakes* on the next page to make sure you are on the right track.

Common Resume Mistakes Checklist

✓ Is the resume too wordy? Have I edited statements down to a few words, powerful words, short words?

✓ Is the layout attractive and *open*, with enough white space?

✓ Is my Job Objective specific? Short enough?

✓ Have I checked the spelling of difficult words?

✓ Are my job-description phrases action-oriented? Have I included *results* and *accomplishments*? Have I used *numbers* and *percentages* wherever possible to show *real* results?

✓ Have I given too much information (such as company address, phone number, supervisor's name, titles, ZIP codes, and so on?)

✓ Does the layout I'm planning to use *flow*? Or does it *jerk* and dart from one part of the page to another?

✓ Does the information sound like I am bragging about myself, rather than presenting hard facts and undoctored information?

✓ Have I correctly removed all proper names that show a political, religious, or philosophical preference?

✓ Have I listed a proper number of schools, rather than too many?

✓ Have I compressed my old jobs into a small space, rather than telling about them in detail?

✓ Have I listed too many part-time jobs separately, instead of more appropriately grouping them together?

✓ Have I given too much information, expecting the reader to pick out what is most important, rather than editing down to a suitable length?

✓ Have I kept the length down to two pages, or in the most extreme case, three—including sufficient white space on each page?

✓ Have I converted highly technical language into easy-to-understand and easy-to-read words, based on the person who will be reading and reviewing this document?

Now, check the following elements that give your resume readability.

Test For Readability

✓ Upper- and lower-case letters, not all-capital letters.

✓ Serif typeface.

✓ Use of bullets where appropriate (periods, followed by 3-4 spaces, followed by an item or phrase).

✓ Adequate leading, or spacing, between lines or items or job descriptions or sections.

✓ Plenty of white space for a clean look.

✓ Wide margins (1 inch on each side, and at top and bottom).

✓ No hyphenated words, no split phrases.

✓ Indentations consistent and used where necessary for clarity.

✓ Proper names of more than one word kept on same line.

✓ Columnar format for body of resume, with maximum width of 3-1/2 to 4-1/2 inches.

✓ Short paragraphs.

✓ Short words.

✓ Phrases, not sentences.

✓ Phrases that begin with action verbs.

✓ Short phrases or sentences, if necessary, throughout.

✓ Upper-left to lower-right *flow*

✓ Few or no abbreviations, and very careful use of them.

You're On Your Way

If you've followed the hints given here, you're well on your way to having a resume that will not only be read, but also *admired*.

People who will be reading, and screening, your resume may or may not be resume experts themselves. In fact, they may know little about resumes. They may even be reading groups of resumes for the first time.

But even those who are new at the job *know what they like to read*. If you've followed my advice so far, that's what you're giving them.

In the next chapter you will learn about another important element of the job search, *letters*. They're more important than most job seekers think.

Writing resumes isn't exactly fun for most of us. And when we're done, we don't look forward to writing a letter to accompany the resume. We'd rather *not* write for awhile.

But sometimes the cover letter is even *more* important than the resume itself.

Chapter 7
The Cover Letter

The Cover Letter Is Your Introduction

The cover letter accompanies a resume and is its proper "companion."

The resume might be thought of as "needing an introduction." You may do this introduction yourself, in person. Or someone else, perhaps a friend who works at the organization, may do it for you. Or the cover letter can serve as your "introduction."

But you *do* need an introduction. Don't just attempt to "barge your way in."

Cover letters provide an opportunity to deliver a more personalized message to the recipient; the resume itself is usually produced in quantity—25, 50, 100 or so—and there is little chance to customize each one for individual employers.

But the cover letter provides the perfect place to do this customizing, to make the communication a personal one between employer and applicant.

Your cover letter should always be typed, on a very fine quality office-type typewriter . . . or on a letter-quality or laser-based computer printer.

It would be foolish to prepare a first quality resume and then to include with it a cover letter typed on an old home-portable typewriter . . . or on a dot-matrix computer printer.

Do it right! Doing it right also means that you *never* mass produce a cover letter. Cover letters are individually prepared, individually written, individually typed or printed, and the material in it should be aimed directly at the target . . . the market . . . the recipient.

Cover letters which begin "To Whom It May Concern:" or "Good Morning," or "Dear Sir or Madam:" are as incorrect as an uninvited guest at a formal party.

Impersonal letters are not given a warm reception by employer. They may, indeed, be treated the same way as you treat mass-produced advertising materials you receive in the mail.

They go into the wastebasket!

Don't Send Cover Letters To Strangers

Because the cover letter is a personal form of correspondence, you should use the name of the person who will receive the letter. Learn it, and then spell it correctly.

If you are using the cover letter to send a resume as a follow-up on a phone conversation or after a face-to-face meeting, you will ruin a wonderful opportunity if you misspell the name, title, the name of the organization, or even a word within the letter.

In a cover letter, you have the opportunity to be personal and specific . . . and to highlight something which may be directly related to the specific job in question . . . and which you may have neglected in the resume itself.

It also provides an opportunity to *repeat* something *from* the resume, but which may be "buried" toward the end, or in the middle and would not be immediately noticeable.

The Golden Rule For Job Hunters

Always go through the back door. Get to know someone who works at the organization. Use her or his name to get in personal contact with someone in the department you hope to work for.

If you take the time and trouble to learn the name, and make the acquaintance of, someone who works at the organization, you will gain a *tremendous* advantage!

Do not break this rule! Letters from strangers rarely receive much attention. Phone calls almost never do. But phone calls or letters from *friends*—or from *friends of friends*—get attention!

Would you ever turn away the friend of a respected personal friend, or of a business colleague, who came to you for advice?

Of course not. And neither would the potential employers you contact.

The Network Advantage

Your network consists of the people you know, and the people *they* know . . . and the people *all* of *them* know. So, within a phone call or two, *you* can tie into this vast "network."

For job hunters, your personal network is of great importance.

What if you don't know anyone in the organization you're targeting and hope to work for?

Use your network! Use, and continue using, the names of people you know, and the people *they* know, to get the name of someone working in the organization, or in the field of work you hope to enter.

But what if you don't think anyone in your network of contacts knows anyone there, either? Should you conclude that you're "out in the cold" and must use the front door?

No! Don't give up so quickly.

Through your network, you can *always* find the name of someone in the organization. Simply keep looking! It may take a few extra hours or a few more phone calls. (Some of them may be long-distance calls, so be prepared!) But if you keep looking, you will find the access route to your contact.

Tips On Writing A Good Cover Letter

Write To A Person, Not To A Title

Use your network to get the name. Then use it. In your opening paragraph, use the name of the person who referred you.

A colleague of mine, a prominent executive recruiter in the East, receives hundreds of unsolicited, unwanted resumes annually. He responds only to those who use the name of someone he knows. In these situations it becomes a matter of good manners to respond to a "friend of a friend."

Your cover letter should be addressed to the person who has the power to hire you! This is most likely the person who manages the department where you want to work.

And that is *not* the Personnel Director.

Surprisingly, most Personnel Directors have the power to reject candidates, but not to hire them.

Have A Strong Opening Statement

Open with a strong positive statement about yourself and your qualifications.

Or simply say that you have been advised to write by Mr. Michael Sanborn (or whomever), the addressee's friend or acquaintance (and a part of your network).

If you have the name of a mutual friend, colleague, or acquaintance, use it first. If you do not, start off with your *best* selling point. Then give the name of the position you are aiming for.

Here are some examples of good opening lines:

> *"I recently graduated from Paramount Business College with a 3.75 grade average and received my Associate Degree in Secretarial Science and Office Management."*

> *"Enclosed is my resume for your advertised position of Assistant Cook."*

> *"I recently graduated form Johnson County Community College with a Diploma in Food Service and have worked successfully as a cook for Bob's Big Boy on Wallace Avenue for the past two years."*

> *"Your advertisement in The Tribune for a Computer Programmer seems to match my qualifications exactly."*

> *"I have two years of experience as an Operator/Programmer with L. G. Williams, Inc., and have now completed my Certificate in Data Processing courses."*

> *"After five years of successful experience in a similar position in Portland, I am enclosing my application for the Community Development Officer position."*

> *"This sounds like the job I have been waiting for! It appears to match the qualifications gained in my seven years of social work experience."*

A good opening statement grabs attention without turning off the reader. It helps to "categorize" your application in the event that the organization is advertising several openings.

If you do not have a very *specific* opening line in your cover letter, your resume might end up in the wrong place, or in the wrong hands. Or it could take a long time to reach the right person as it floats through the various departments of a large organization.

Each person who receives your resume (by mistake!) will send it on to someone else (who may also be uninterested in it or may be the wrong person to be receiving it!).

Sometimes, someone along the line will "file it." If this happens, you're "dead in the water," and you will probably never hear from anyone in that organization again.

Or they may destroy it or toss it away, deciding not to route it further. And you're dead again!

So you must do whatever you can to keep your resume alive, and to get it onto someone's desk who has the power to make a hiring decision for someone like you.

Keep Your Letter Short, Make It Look Good, And Include Key Strengths

How long should a cover letter be? Keep it on *one page*. And the body of your cover letter should occupy *no more* than about 50 percent of the page.

Use plenty of white space. Keep your sentences short, your paragraphs short, and design your letter so that it looks inviting and easy to read. If you do not, it may not be read at all!

Write several drafts! Edit your letter as carefully as you do your resume. It must be perfect!

It should be tailored as closely as you know how, to the recipient's needs and requirements, as best you know them.

To do this, highlight the best items from your background which directly qualify you for the job. Bring out your strong points . . . the things someone might miss in the resume itself.

Your objective is to arouse the reader's interest immediately, with something directly related, very *interesting* . . . and very attractively presented in an easy-to-read format.

Signing Your Cover Letter

When signing your typewritten cover letter, type your *real* name. If you wish, sign your nickname, or the name by which you like to be called. But type your full name, first and last. (Skip your middle initial; using it can sound a bit arrogant.)

If your name is Paul Charleston Bosworth, Jr., and if they call you "Chuck," and if your formal written name is P. Charleston Bosworth, type Charleston Bosworth, then sign it "Chuck Bosworth." If you are known as Charles, sign it that way.

Sample Cover Letters

Most cover letters follow a standard outline:

- The first paragraph states your strongest point(s) and the job for which you want to be considered.

- The second paragraph states why you want to work for this organization (talk about them, not about yourself!)

- The third paragraph highlights skills and qualifications from your resume that are relevant to that particular organization.

- The fourth paragraph requests an interview and suggests how you will follow up.

Here are two examples of good cover letters.

4550 Parrier Street
Espinosa, California
April 20, 19XX

Mr. Craig Schmidt
District Manager
Desert Chicken Shops
P. O. Box 6230
Los Angeles, California 98865

Dear Mr. Schmidt,

My resume (enclosed) outlines my four years of successful experience as a fast food manager with a nationwide network of restaurants. I graduated from a Restaurant Management curriculum at Harman University with a 3.75 GPA in 1985.

I have been impressed with the rapid growth and exceptional quality of product and service for which Desert Chicken has become well known. This is the kind of organization I hope to work for.

My experience includes positions as cook, night manager, assistant manager and as manager for my current employer.

I will call your office in a few days to see if we might schedule a convenient time to meet and discuss some areas of mutual interest.

Thanks very much for your consideration.

Sincerely,

Douglas Parker

Douglas Parker

6345 Highland Boulevard
Minneapolis, Minnesota 55066
July 10, 19XX

Mr. James A. Blackwell
Vice President, Engineering
Acme Revolving Door Company
New Brunswick, Pennsylvania 21990

Dear Mr. Blackwell:

I graduated from the University of Minnesota this spring
with a 3.66 grade average and a Bachelor of Science Degree
in Mechanical Engineering.

Your company has been highly recommended to me by my
uncle, John Blair, the Pennsylvania District Governor for
Rotary, International. He has appreciated your friendship
and business relationship over the years and has advised me
to forward my resume.

My own reading in business publications has kept me aware
of the new products which Acme has marketed.

My objective is to design mechanical parts for a privately
owned company which enjoys an excellent reputation and
which conducts business internationally.

I hope that I may take the liberty of calling your office to
see if we might meet to discuss possible opportunities with
Acme. I plan to be in Pennsylvania toward the end of next
month, and this might provide a convenient time to meet, if
your schedule permits.

Sincerely,

Patricia Dugan

Patricia Dugan
Home phone number: (612) 555-3445

Enclosed: resume

Most writers of cover letters make one major mistake above all others. It comes in the closing paragraph.

It is so common that some books written by well-known resume authorities show it as "the correct way." It is not correct.

The mistake is this: In the closing paragraph, the writer mistakenly says:

> *"My home telephone number is 000-0000, and I may be reached there between the hours of 4 and 6 P.M. daily. Please call me to arrange an interview."*

In the minds of knowledgeable people, this is a signal that the writer is *lazy*. Why? Because it says:

> *"I'm at home, and I want you to call me if you are interested."*

Instead, I recommend that you say you'll call, that you *do* call, and that you *continue* to call, until you get through.

If they are truly eager to call you, they have your number on a resume, or can find it easily enough at the bottom of your letter.

But by your willingness to call, you show a sense of interest, enthusiasm and willingness to work that the "you call me" letter writer will never be able to imply.

Other Types Of Cover Letters

Broadcast Letters

A broadcast letter is a combination cover letter and resume. It is a special letter, directed to a specific person, someone who is the chief executive officer (CEO), a vice-president or other ranking executive of an organization.

It is sometimes called a Marketing Letter, because it is used as a part of the "marketing myself" job-hunting campaign.

Some companies specialize in writing a Broadcast Letter for you, typing these in quantity, and sending them out to appropriate executives in your chosen field. The fee for composing, printing, and sending these letters can be substantial.

I know of some firms which charge hundreds, even thousands of dollars, for this service. Is it worth the cost? I think not.

Do they work? My opinion is that they do not work well enough to justify the cost for most people. If you wish to consider this technique, read Carl Boll's book, *Executive Jobs Unlimited*, generally considered to be the best book on Broadcast Letters.

Advocates of the Marketing, or Broadcast, Letter claim that it pulls inquiries and responses at double or triple the rate which one can expect when using unsolicited resumes and cover letters.

But resumes and cover letters often pull just one to two percent response, and that means that Broadcast Letters would pull four to six percent at the very best.

The primary advantage of Broadcast/Marketing Letters may just lie in the fact that they are professionally prepared, professionally typed and printed, and *targeted* directly at the leading executives in your field.

Resumes, when sent blindly to personnel offices and recruiters, in quantities large and small, could not be expected to work as well as cleverly-targeted Broadcast Letters.

But otherwise, the difference is usually insignificant.

Responding To Want Ads

When you respond to a "help wanted" advertisement, don't expect miracles.

If an ad lists the name of the employer, an address, phone number, and more, you have a reasonable chance at receiving a reply. But don't hold your breath.

Thousands of people will be reading the very same ad, and many employers are overloaded with responses.

Chapter 8

Saying Thank-You & Following Up

The Impact Of Good Manners And Thank-You Notes

Good manners are an important part of the job hunt.

Doing the right thing at the right time will help you get the right job. Failing to do the right thing may well result in your being eliminated along the way, or rejected.

Final selection of the winner from among a group of equally-qualified candidates is most often made on "feel," on "fit," and on "how they will get along here."

Well-mannered people who communicate *by their actions* their knowledge of what to do and how to handle social situations, have a major advantage over others who fail to demonstrate such knowledge.

In this chapter, you will learn some of the right techniques to display good manners in the job hunt . . . and the correct methods for implementing those techniques.

Thanking People In Your Life

Thanking people is probably the most important factor in the category of good manners. Everyone likes to be thanked.

But usually, job hunters and job applicants are so focused on their *own* problems, strategies, tactics and activities that they fail to apply good manners as a strategy throughout the job search process.

They are *the* most important factor. Focusing on the other person and treating that person with courtesy, manners and thoughtfulness will do wonders for increasing the opportunities for success in your job hunt.

Job applicants should *follow through* after an interview. The first step in that *follow through* procedure is to thank the person who interviewed you.

When you're given a gift, you thank the giver. In an interview, you have been given:

- The *time* of the interviewer;
- The *hospitality* of the receptionist, the interviewer and perhaps others;
- The *consideration* of the organization to be hired as an employee;
- The *information* you received in the interview; and
- The *opportunity* to possibly be hired and to take an important step in your career.

Sequence of Typical Job Hunting Situation

The usual sequence of a job hunting situation:

- An advertisement appears, or you hear of an opening.
- You make a phone call to the organization.
- You submit a resume, cover letter and possibly examples of your work.
- You receive an interview appointment (or a rejection).
- You receive an interview.
- The employer may follow up with a letter or phone call.
- If you have been successful, you are probably asked for a second interview.
- You receive a final offer or polite rejection from the employer.

What's wrong with this "usual scenario?"

You have little or nothing to say about its outcome! That means that results will happen *without* your having anything to say about how things turn out.

That, friends, is where good manners count most. They will provide you with that "extra something" so that you will have a major impact on the outcome . . . and on making that outcome the one *you* want!

How do you do that? It's easy! At the appropriate times, you should respond to an employer's kindness with thank-you notes or cards.

What *are* the appropriate times? They might be situations such as these:

- After the initial phone call to employers, thank them for their kindness and information.
- After the interview, thank them for their time, tour, information, etc.
- After a job offer, thank the initial interviewer and the manager of the department in which you will work.
- After a rejection, thank them for whatever you can . . . something which was positive and helpful for you in their interview and consideration process.

Send Thank-You Notes Or Cards

There are many good reasons to send thank-you notes. Among them:

- You'll feel good when you do.
- The recipient will feel even better than you do.
- It's good manners to do so.
- The recipient will be reminded of you, will think better of you, and will subconsciously be aware of the fact that you "know what to do in social situations."

If an interviewer or manager interviews a few people daily (some interviewers do as many as fifteen interviews on every interview day . . . some as many as thirty! . . . and it is definitely, by that time, *not* fun for them to see another applicant), it is important to do whatever you can to be remembered in a positive manner.

Thank-you notes or cards are the easiest, most inexpensive way to do this.

Choosing Notes, Cards Or Stationery—Size, Style And Color

You will find cards in the stores with "Thank-you" printed, engraved or embossed thereon.

You'll see other note cards which are plain. Some have borders, some do not. You'll discover that a wide variety of colors is available.

Choose a conservative style, not a loud, wild, or unusual one. Stay away from patterns, illustrations, or trendy designs.

Thank-you notes or plain notes are usually smaller than personal-size stationery and much smaller than business stationery.

Should you use the personalized stationery which you already own? Probably not. For this special occasion, use something special, something better than ordinary paper which is used for ordinary correspondence. If, however, you happen to have fine quality paper with superior printing or engraving, and if you know about things like this because of your background, go right ahead and use them. If they are not "the best," however, buy something more distinctive and appropriate.

Choose a plain color, such as white, off-white, cream, ivory, or very light gray. Don't select dark or pastel colors since these are not considered businesslike.

Write your message, a short one, on the bottom part of the inside panel, the one on the bottom after you open the card. If you must, or if your writing is large, you may start at the top, and then write on both the top and bottom panels. Do not continue onto the back side.

Do I Write? Or Print? Or Type?

Thank-you notes, cards and other personal styles of correspondence should be personally written. If your handwriting is good, use it.

How do you know if your writing is good enough? If people occasionally compliment you on your handwriting, it is probably good enough; if they do not, be cautious about writing by hand.

If it isn't good, you have a decision to make. The next best thing, then, for you to do is to *print* your thank-you. If both your handwriting *and* your printing are terrible, you should type it.

But don't type on the notes we've been discussing. Save your typing for business-size stationery (8-1/2" x 11").

Some Tips On Writing Good Thank-You Notes

Here are some tips which should help you to be #1!

- **DO.** Address the note "Dear Mr. or Ms." rather than using his or her first name. This is proper even if the interviewer has invited you to call him or her by a first name. Obviously, if the interviewer is a personal friend or acquaintance of you and your family, and if you have known the person for years, you may use whatever name you normally call the person, if you feel comfortable in doing so for this business situation.

- **DO.** Keep your note short. This is *not* the time to rehash everything you discussed in an interview, nor is it the time to bring up something you had previously neglected to mention.

- **DO.** Write about something special, if you can. Bring up something which relates specifically to *you* and to *your* interview which may not relate to all the other applicants.

- **DO.** Spell everything correctly. One misspelled word could torpedo your chances. If you're not a good speller, (many otherwise-bright people are not!) check each word of your spelling with a dictionary or with a friend who is a "born speller."

- **DO.** Time your thank-you note to arrive on a good day. How can you know this? If the interviewer tells you they'll be talking to candidates over the next three weeks, wait a few days before mailing it. If they will make the decision in 48 hours, you should write the note immediately and take it to a postal facility where it will be processed within a few hours. Or drop it off yourself.

- **DO.** Put your return address on the envelope. On a small envelope, it belongs on the back; on a business envelope, it can be written on the back or in the upper left-hand corner of the front side.

- **DO.** Put adequate postage on the envelope. If you don't, it may result in your envelope being returned to you (a possibly fatal delay!) or in the post office generously deciding to deliver it "postage due," which the employer will not smile about.

- **DO.** Use an attractive commemorative postage stamp. Studies prove that attractive stamps used in direct-mail advertising result in greater sales. Do *not* use a postage meter for personal correspondence. This is not only improper, but it may lead the recipient to conclude that you may be using "company postage for your personal use."

- **DON'T.** Use politically-controversial stamps, either for postage or for decoration or for sealing the flap on the reverse side. The person opening your letter may not be as interested in "Free South Africans" as you are.

- **DO.** Use a good quality pen, with a business-color ink, preferably dark blue or black.

- **DON'T.** Oversell yourself! The purpose of this note, card or letter is to thank, not to sell. Avoid cliches such as:

  I'm the best person to do this job!

  Hire me, and you'll never be sorry.

  I'm inexperienced, but I'm eager!

  I'll work for nothing if you only give me a chance!

  Please give me this job. I need it!

- **DO.** Sign your formal name or your conversational name, the name you were called in the interview when writing a note by hand.

- **DO.** Type your formal name, then sign your conversational name if you are typing a letter.

Some Sample Thank-You Notes

Here are a few sample notes and letters for you to use for ideas when you compose your own.

April 22, 19XX

Dear Mr. Nelson,

Thanks so much for seeing me while I was in town last week. I appreciate your kindness, the interview, and all the information you gave me.

I will call you once again in a few weeks to see if any openings have developed in your marketing research department's planned expansion.

Appreciatively,

Phil Simmons

Phil Simmons

(after a phone call, before an interview)

September 17, 19XX

Mr. Bill Kenner
Sales Manager
WRTV
Rochester, Minnesota

Dear Mr. Kenner:

Thank you very much for the interview and the market information you gave me yesterday. I was most impressed with the city, with your station, and with everyone I met.

As you requested, I am enclosing a resume and have requested that my ex-manager call you on Tuesday, the 21st at 10:00 a.m.

Working at WRTV with you and your team would be both interesting and exciting for me. I look forward to your reply and to the possibility of helping you set new records for next year.

Sincerely,

Anne Bently

Anne Bently
1434 River Drive
Polo, Washington 99654

October 14, 19XX

Dear Bill,

I really appreciate your recommending me to Alan Stevens at Wexler Cadillac.

We met yesterday for almost an hour, and we're having lunch again Friday.

If this develops into a job offer, as I think it may, I will be most grateful.

Enclosed is a copy of a reference letter by my summer employer. I thought you might find it helpful.

You're a good friend, and I appreciate your thinking of me.

Sincerely,

Dave

Dave

July 26, 19XX

Dear Ms. Bailey,

Thank you for the interview for the auditor's job last week.

I appreciate the information you gave me and the opportunity to interview with John Peters. He asked me for a transcript, which I am forwarding today.

Working in my field of finance in a respected firm such as Barry Productions appeals to me greatly.

I appreaciate your consideration and look forward to hearing from you.

Sincerely,

Dan Rehling

Dan Rehling

May 21, 19XX

Ms. Sandra Waller
Yellow Side Stores
778 Northwest Boulevard
Seattle, Washington 99659

Dear Ms. Waller:

Thank you so much for the interview you gave me last Friday for the Retail Mangement Training Program. I learned a great deal and know now that retailing is my first choice for a career.
I am looking forward to interviewing with Mr. Daniel and Ms. Sobczak next week.

For that meeting, I will bring two copies of my resume and a transcript, as you suggested.

Enclosed is a copy of a reference letter written by my summer employer. I thought you might find it helpful.

Sincerely,

Elizabeth Duncan

March 22, 19XX

Dear Ms. Samson,

Thanks for talking with me by phone today. You made me feel at ease!

I appreciate your granting me an interview appointment and will look forward to meeting you in your office at 10:00 a.m. on Tuesday, March 29.

I will bring my design portfolio with me. Thanks again.

Sincerely,

Bradley Kurtz

Follow-Up!

Have you ever been disappointed with the actions, or inactions of other people . . . or with their dependability, or their undependability?

Of course! That is the way most people lead their lives, and that is exactly the way most people conduct their job hunt.

They fail to take responsibility to follow up, to follow through, and to do what they say they will do.

Imagine what possibilities arise when you do things which other people fail to do . . . which other candidates-for-employment fail to do . . . and which employers themselves would never imagine that candidates would do!

Follow up. Follow through. Do what others do not do. Do what others do not think about doing.

Following Up *Before* An Interview

After you make a phone call to an employer, when that employer has invited you to an interview, you might use one of these methods to follow through:

- Write a confirming letter or note of thanks and restating the time when you will be there.

- Call the person's assistant or secretary, probably one or two days prior to the date of the interview, inquiring whether the time is still convenient, and to ask any other questions you may have (for example, travel directions).

Do not call the person with whom you will be interviewing. This would be considered "overkill" and might create a negative "who does this person think he (or she) is?" impression.

Following Up *After* An Interview

Send a thank-you note, of course. Be certain it creates a good impression and that it is appropriate, both to you and to the situation.

Do not include any other information with the thank-you note. That would be considered "mixing business activities with personal activities."

Other material (transcripts, reference letters, photocopies of credentials, etc.) should be sent separately, in a larger envelope. These things should always be accompanied by some type of correspondence, even if it is only a Post-It Note or a short letter of transmittal.

Following Up After Being Rejected

Should you follow up after being rejected? Logic, common sense and your own personal pride all tell you, "*no!*"

This isn't necessarily true. In fact, if you are being creative in your job hunt, you will think "possibility," not "no possibility." Failing to contact the employer is "no possibility" thinking.

Those who *do* follow up often do so for the wrong reason: to find out why they were rejected. To find out what they did "wrong."

Will most employers tell them where they went wrong? No. And rarely will they tell the *whole* truth. After all, it isn't always in an employer's best interest to tell someone that he or she had bad breath, body odor, wore dirty clothes, had dirty hair, wasn't appropriately dressed, had bad taste or displayed poor manners.

So when you do follow up after being rejected, do this:

- Thank the employer for the interviewing process (again); for the consideration you received (again); for any additional materials, interviews, meals, hospitality you have received since your first written thank-you . . . and that's all.

- Then, to open the domain of "possibility" for yourself, restate your interest in other opportunities in the organization for yourself. Restate this in *one* sentence, in a very enthusiastic manner, but don't do it *at length*. Keep it short!

- Finally, close with a "possibility" statement, such as "I would like the opportunity to stay in touch with you over the next few months. Thanks very much for everything."

This allows you the option you want. Instead of the door being closed, it is now open.

"What good will this do me?"

Perhaps none. But perhaps much. I know cases where a reopened door led to an immediate reconsideration of the candidate: "If he really liked us that much, maybe we should hire him."

Or it left the door open, so that when the organization's first-choice candidate rejected the offer she received, the possibility had already been created to call their second choice, the person who "is so interested in us that she sent a letter restating how enthusiastic she is about us."

Following Up With Your Network

Every few weeks, it's a good idea to follow up, in writing or by phone, with important people in your network.

Following up means staying in touch with them, not to see if they can do anything for you. And not to see if they have done anything for you.

It means staying in touch to see how they are, to inquire about how their family is, or how their organization's sales or services are coming along, and perhaps to thank them for anything they might have done for you or for any advice they may have given along the way.

If what they have done is to provide support for you, to be "thinking positively for you toward the possibility of getting the job and the opportunity you want," then the purpose for your call or note is to acknowledge them for that support.

Your contact with them might take other forms. Try one or more of these in your stay-in-touch-with-your network plan:

- Send a magazine article which interests you and which would definitely interest them.

- Send an article which interests them, but which holds no interest for you.

- Send a cartoon or a few cartoons or jokes (in good taste, please!) which are likely to produce a smile or a laugh from them.

- Call with some new information which you have uncovered about a topic which interests him or her, or which interests both of you.

By staying in touch, perhaps every few weeks, and by being *focused on the other person*, rather than on your own needs and wants, you will achieve what you want.

What you want . . . is for the recipient to think, if only for few seconds, or moments, about you . . . to think about what a nice person you are . . . and about the possibility that they might be able to help or respond to you in some way.

Following Up And Staying In Control

During your job hunt, *you* should remain in control.

Most job hunters think they have no control. They think "circumstances" have control . . . that "employers" are in control . . . that "the organizations" have the power and the control.

But organizations exist only because people are in them and because often people need to be served by them. And you, friend, are those "people." So you *have* the control.

In the job hunt, you must not give up all control.

One of the major mistakes is to expect employers to call you, rather than your calling them. Most cover letters conclude with "My number is 000-0000, and I may be reached between X a.m. and X p.m."

The moment they are requested to be calling you, rather than your calling them, you've lost control.

Waiting for the telephone to ring is not part of your job hunt campaign. It puts you *out* of control. It prevents you from being *pro*-active and requires you to be *re*-active.

In your letter, say that *you* will call. In the interview, thank them for offering to call, but ask if you might call them instead.

When you call, you may not get through. Call again. Continue to call until you get through. Leave your name, but never leave your number.

When you leave your number, you've lost control.

After several unsuccessful attempts to talk to the person you want to reach, you might consider asking, "When is a good time to reach her for a one-minute phone conversation? I've tried different times and haven't had much luck?"

Following Up By Creating The Environment

When you call back, as opposed to someone else calling, you have an opportunity to *create the environment* for your call.

If they call you, your kids may be screaming. Or you may be testing the *loudness* control on your stereo. Or your dog may be barking. Even worse, you may be in an argument with someone and be in a mood which you would prefer others not to know about.

When you call them, create a *quiet* environment. Focus on them, on what you will say, on being alert and pleasant, and on eliminating possibilities for a negative environment:

- Send the kids outside.
- Turn off the radio and the stereo.
- Turn off the TV!
- Have paper and pen handy.
- Be in sight of the door, so that you can see and be warned about approaching visitors.
- Don't be eating, drinking or chewing gum.
- Have a glass of water handy, in case you need it.
- Be clear about the purposes of your call—use notes written down about what you will say, what questions you want answered.
- Ask if the person you reach "has a minute or two to talk right now?"
- Always give your name slowly, clearly, distinctly. Remind them of who you are, what you were in their office for, and do it all slowly!
- Smile! Keep both your physical and your mental selves *happy*!
- When you conclude, stay in control. If someone tells you, "we'll call you if we get anything," ask if you might call them again sometime, "because I'm gone quite a bit." Then call again or write again, to stay in touch and to find out about them, not about what is coming up for you.

Keep Smiling

In the course of following up and following through, you'll be rejected. You won't get through. You won't be acknowledged for the wonderful person you are.

Whatever happens, keep smiling!

Whatever your problems may be, don't talk about them. Remember: they're not particularly interested in yours. They're interested in their own.

So focus on them. And sound happy, enthusiastic, and pleasant. Not eager, not pushy, not needing or wanting . . . just happy and competent.

So S-M-I-L-E, and you'll come across the way you want to come across.

Chapter 9

Job
Search
Tips

Additional Tips For Your Job Search

In this book, I've provided a variety of ways to help you create a resume which will be attractive-to-the-eye, easy-to-read, easy-to-skim, elegant-to-touch, and which contains the kind of substance employers are looking for when selecting new employees.

But your resume is for your job search. So here is a review of the job search advice given throughout this book as well as a few new tips.

Private And State Employment Services

Private employment agencies fill a small percentage of jobs filled annually throughout North America.

Some experts say the number is as low as 2 percent or 5 percent.

One five-person agency in a medium-sized American city of 600,000 people placed a total of 26 people in 1987. From this small amount of activity/results, all five people made a living and supported their families.

The numbers required to "be successful" as a placement person in a private employment agency are *much* smaller than you might expect.

What are your odds, then? Small. Very small. Slight. Very slight.

Should you, then, give up on agencies?

No. But give them what they deserve: a small amount of your time. . . and do *not* depend on them.

The State Employment Services

The 50 employment services, one in each state, and the similar organizations in Canada, in each province, are also known as "the unemployment offices" in most states and provinces.

The name might be appropriate. Unemployment compensation checks and applications are handled in another department, but the term "unemployment" fits more often than "employment."

Should you give up on state or provincial employment offices?

Probably. They may be worth a small amount of your time. But not much.

One study quoted in *"What Color Is Your Parachute?"* shows that most people placed (relatively few *are* placed from the large pool of applicants received by these government offices) were not working at their new jobs after just thirty days!

So the offices, while they *did* place some of their applicants, were, in effect, acting as "temporary help agencies," i.e., placing people on jobs where they remained for only a short time.

Don't depend on them.

Personnel Offices

When I was Corporate Director of Personnel, in charge of all recruiting, screening and hiring, I thought that those three activities constituted "what I did for a living" and "what I do at work."

Wrong.

What I did at work was to:

- Recruit large numbers of people for jobs.

- Eliminate large numbers of people from consideration for jobs.

- Send final candidates to department heads for further screening out and semi-rejection from our view, permanent and final rejection from each candidate's view.

- Ultimately reject all but one candidate for each job.

What I really *did*, then, was to spend *most* of my time *rejecting* candidates.

So although my title was OK and acceptable, what I actually *did*, from most people's point of view, is now deemed UNacceptable.

That is, when I admit to people, now, that my primary duty, that the activity in which I spent a majority of my time . . . was that of *rejection*, those people utter some quite-nasty remarks:

- "Don't you think that was unfair?"
- "Didn't you miss some awfully good candidates for employment if you stopped reading resumes after you had 'enough good ones to pick from?'"
- "If you were looking for *reasons to reject candidates*, wasn't your attitude quite negative?"
- "Why didn't you look for the good things, rather than the bad things?"

We do, of course, look for the good things.

All interviewers, screeners, recruiters and personnel people look for the best traits we can find in people.

We first screen-in the qualified people, those who possess the required technical knowledge and the educational background which we have determined, or which someone in the department which is going to do the *work* has determined, is the *first* thing we will require.

But once we get enough of those candidates, then we must look for things which will eliminate *some* of those from the running.

And when one is looking for reasons to eliminate people, those reasons are usually negative ones.

> *ASIDE: By not even considering some people with less-than-the-minimum experience or educational background, aren't we, **again**, missing the possibility of some excellent candidates?*

Yes. Of course, we are! But we can't see *everyone*.

We can see only a few. So, unfair as it is, we draw lines. Some people get in. Others are left out.

Understand that personnel offices deal with *many* people. Sometimes, they lose their cool. Sometimes, they don't treat you fairly. Sometimes, they seem to act as though they don't even care if you get a job there or not. Sometimes, they aren't polite. Sometimes, they forget who you are. Sometimes, they goof up and fail to write you, or to call you, or to invite you.

Bounce back.

Understand those things, and then go on with dealing with the office.

Or, if you want my best advice, avoiding dealing with them completely.

After all, they are in the *rejection business*, not the *hiring business*.

The person in the *hiring business* is the one who gets to see the *few* candidates after the Personnel Department *rejects* the *many* candidates.

So if you can eliminate the step called The Personnel Department, or the Personnel Interview, or The Screening Interview, or The Initial Interview, do so!

> **ASIDE:** *In recent years, the numbers of large companies have been decreasing, and the numbers of small companies have been increasing.*

Studies show that most job opportunities, most *new* jobs created in our fast-moving, fast-changing economy, come from organizations which have 100 employees or fewer, and that most of those jobs come from organizations which have fewer than 20 employees.

And more than 2/3 of our workers, nationwide, in the USA, now work in "small businesses," i.e., companies which have fewer than 250 employees.

When you next read about plans being made for large companies, notice this: those plans most always include "downsizing," rather than "increasing the number of employees."

Do these smaller companies *have* Personnel Departments?

No.

Most do not. This is especially true of the 20-or-fewer category, but it is true of the 100-or-fewer and even of the 250-or-fewer, too.

In these firms, managers, executives, and line-management people do the selecting and hiring, rather than staff people, in a Personnel or Human Resources Department.

Use your networking abilities to get to know someone in the field, in the company, in the city, in a church, who can get you to the person who is in *charge of hiring* . . . and forget about trying to see the person who is in *charge of rejection.*

And do not stop until you get to know who they are, until you get to meet or talk with them, and until you get the opportunity to present yourself, *very carefully*, in person.

That, my friends, is the way people get hired . . . and the way people avoid being summarily rejected.

Applications

If you do go through The Personnel Department, do so carefully.

Be nice, even if they are not.

Be well-dressed, neat and clean, even if they are not.

Be on time, even if they are not.

Be well-prepared and know about their organization, even if they appear to know nothing about you . . . and appear to care even less.

Do whatever you must to be certain you are *the #1 candidate* when you present yourself at, in, or through The Personnel Department.

Remember, the person there is not seeing only "you." They are, at the same moment, comparing you to "all the others."

And before you get angry about this, remember that YOU do it, too, or . . . at least, you DID, when you were dating, or choosing friends, or choosing a church, or selecting a TV.

We all do it.

So just *understand* that "WE ALL DO IT," and be the best-prepared candidate you can be.

Be Prepared

When you go to The Personnel Department, prepare beforehand.

- Read about the organization. Don't complain that you can't; just do it.

- Scout the route. Know how you'll get there and how long it will take. Half an hour early is fine, but 1 minute late is *deadly*.

- Be nice to the greeter/receptionist. Those people have more power in their little finger, or in their writing hand, or in one or two words spoken to the interviewer, than you have, even if you made $250,000 last year!

- Be well-dressed. Not adequately dressed, but well-dressed. The #1 candidate is never hired because he or she is "adequate."

- Be at ease. If you know the organization, or have read about it, you'll be closer to being at ease than if you have no knowledge.

- Go to the bathroom before you arrive. If drinking coffee is likely to require your presence in a bathroom, do not drink coffee.

- If you are carrying materials, a portfolio, papers, or credentials with you to the interview, they should be carried in something classy, not something chintzy. If you are using an attache case, it should be relatively slender and not chock-full of stuff. (Thick attache cases are for students who carry their books to class or for door-to-door salespeople.)

- Do not carry cigarettes with you. And do not smoke, either outside or inside the interview room even if you are offered the opportunity to do so. Of those who smoke, few do it well.

- Do not chew gum. Anywhere. Ever.

- Be clean. Fingers, hands, face, hair, body.

- Have your clothes clean. Unwrinkled. Shoes shined.

- Be well-groomed. If you're a male, consider shaving your beard and mustache. If you're a female, look like a female from *"Working Woman"* magazine rather than from *"Glamour"* or *"Vogue."*

- Don't be nervous. Ask your friends if you have nervous or annoying mannerisms, and invite them to be brutal in telling you about it.

- Better to be aware of the problem and to handle it . . . than to be rejected in your ignorance of the matter.

Filling Out Applications

Everyone hates filling out applications.

And once you've filled out a dozen or so, you hate it even more.

Some of them are one page long, and some are eight pages long.

They are *all* "no fun."

But they *are required*.

They are part and parcel of The Personnel Department.

So when you go, go early enough, if you know you will be required to fill out the application.

If your handwriting is bad, *print*. If your printing is bad, print *slowly* and *neatly*. You *can* do it! If you go slowly enough, you *can* make them *neat* and *attractive*. So just *do it*!

Because doing it neatly is *required*.

If you need information about your background which you have not memorized . . . or about your previous employers, including the company names and addresses, and the names of your supervisors, bring those with you. Put them on some sheets of paper which you will then place in your classy carrier, or attache case, or briefcase.

If you dislike the questions on the application, you have several choices.

First, you can get angry about it and not answer them.

But answering them is *required*. So the result of that action will be *rejection*. Rejection-with-anger, by the way, is less productive than *nice rejection*.

Nice Rejection can mean "Possibility." Rejection-with-anger always means "No possibility."

Second, you can become angry, conquer your anger, then become OK with your thoughts, and answer the questions which angered you. So the organization will get the answers they need and you will no longer be angry.

Third, you can decide that you don't want to work for a company which asks those kinds of questions.

In that case, you leave.

This is also called "No possibility."

But it might be a pretty good idea.

Bad Questions on applications can come from intent or from ignorance.

If they come from ignorance, it's no big deal. We're all ignorant once in a while.

But if the Bad Questions come from intent, then perhaps you are in the wrong place for an interview-and-application.

So if you decide to leave, you are opening the space for someone who isn't quite so bright, or discerning, or choosy, or fussy as you are. So be it.

The Last Word On Filling Out Applications

Applications are used for screening people out, just as resumes are.

So fill them out carefully in a manner which will allow you to be *in*, rather than *out*, of consideration.

If the application says "Salary Expected" or "Salary Desired," write the word "*open*." Don't put an amount.

A specific amount can get you *in consideration* very quickly, but for a smaller amount of money than they might otherwise have been willing to pay you . . . before they discovered, the paltry amount you would be willing to work for!

Disclose nothing which you know can eliminate you from being *in consideration*.

Do not be cryptic. Do not say "Personal" in reply to questions.

In short, use common sense. Most job applicants do not. They use Fog Logic, not Clear Logic.

Be clear, and view your application from the employer's point of view, the reader's point of view.

Tell them things which will keep you *in consideration* and which will prevent you from being eliminated.

Common sense? Absolutely.

Commonly done? No.

Be creative. Be clever. Be hired.

The Road Less Traveled: A More Effective Way

Find out what everyone else is doing.

Then do something else.

Something different. Something better. Something creative.

Are there better ways than "the way everyone tells me to do my job hunt?"

As you read in the first chapter, and as some of you have heard, there may be. My feeling is that there *is*.

What you do in your job hunt is a function, of course, of what you already know.

In this book, you learned a very different way to look at resumes. You saw a way that focuses not on *you*, but on the person doing the skimming, the reading and the selecting.

If job applicants are going through the motions of writing a resume, so that they can send out five hundred, so that they can get twelve replies, so that they can get six interviews, so that they can get two offers and then choose between them . . . then those people shouldn't bother with this book.

Neither should they bother with this chapter.

But if you understand *now* that what you *do* in your life and in your job hunt, is a function of what you *know*, then you might be interested in *knowing* a bit more.

Here it is. A set of creative ideas to help your job hunt result in success . . . and in your achieving *aliveness* in the job you land . . . a job you truly love. A job you look forward to. A job you're so eager for, that you'd gladly go there and do it for nothing!

Networking—When It Works And When It Doesn't

Networking, used correctly, can help you achieve exactly what you want.

But only if you *know* exactly what you want.

So before you follow the Yuppie advice and "network yourself like crazy," understand two things:

- Getting help from others in your network requires you to give help to others in your network . . . and to others not currently in your network. Successful living is a give and take situation, and it works better if you give *more* than you take, or expect to take.

- Individuals in your network *want* to help you. But only if you make it relatively easy. And only if you've done your part of the work *first*.

Asking *me* to get *you* a job isn't the idea. Not at all.

But giving me the opportunity to help you, help me, and help a friend of mine: that's the idea of network and networking, applied properly.

Before you network, know what you want to *do*. Know what skills you have. Know what problems those skills can solve. Know the areas in which you would like to apply those skills to solve specific problems.

Know *all* those things.

Then, *only then*, start to call on your network.

First: Friends And Relatives

Call on friends and relatives first. Call especially on people for whom you have done favors.

Let them know your objectives, skills , talents, abilities, and interests.

Then ask them if they know anyone who is *already doing* what you want to do . . . using the skills you plan to use.

It would be nice if that person is applying his or her skills in a field which interests you strongly. But even if that's not the case, even if that person is applying the skills in a field which doesn't interest you at all, take the next step.

The next step is to see if your friend or relative would, on your behalf, arrange a meeting among the three of you; a lunch, an after-work snack or sandwich, a chat at your friend's home, or anything which brings you together socially.

The purpose of the meeting is for you to learn what your contact person is doing and how he or she likes it. Does that person like the place he or she is working, and does he or she know anyone or any organization who is working in the field you're aiming for ... and who may have need for a person with your skills ... or who may have the kinds of problems you're capable of solving.

Then follow up, follow through. Network again to meet the people your contact person knows, and continue to do this.

At each step along the way, *thank* people. Use your good manners. Send notes, even to your relative or friend whom you see regularly.

Thank the third person, the friend-of-your-relative, too. Write a note. Stay in touch. Keep thanking people. Keep validating them . . . helping them know that they count . . . that they've done a good turn.

You'll find that networking works wonders. It can get you into places and into organizations you'd never know about or imagine that you could penetrate.

Most of you got most of *your* jobs through friends, relatives and acquaintances.

So use the strategy to get your next job, too.

twenty-eight percent of all people, at the minimum, get their jobs through friends, relatives and acquaintances.

That's more than twice the number that admit to getting their jobs through a newspaper classified ad.

So if it works twice as well, give it twice the effort.

Develop New "Acquaintances"

It's not only "who you know."

It's who you will take the trouble to meet from now on.

So create a new network. A better network.

If the places you've been going, the people you've been hanging out with, haven't been supporting your goals and objectives to get where you want to go in your life and your career, it might be time to add a new friend or two to the group.

One way to do this, easily, is to get new names, and names of new social organizations, from people you already know. Branch out, just as a tree does. Grow a new branch from one which already exists.

And if you need or want to make a clean break, join new groups. Attend a different church of your denomination. Go to groups as a guest of your friends. Network there, too.

How?

Listen to people. Ask questions of people. Don't pester them to death with talk about yourself.

Listeners go over much bigger than talkers do.

That's especially true for the first few times you meet someone.

Be interested in them, rather than concentrating on impressing them with how interesting you are . . . what you've done . . . where you've been . . . how wonderful you are . . . and especially with "the bad breaks you've had."

Ask questions. Then listen. Agree. Acknowledge. Be interested. (Who knows? You might even learn something!)

The more branches you add to your tree, the better and stronger your network will be.

Get Referrals To Supervisors And Managers, Too

In addition to talking to people who are doing what you want to do, who are using the skills you want to use on a job, don't omit supervisors and managers.

Network your way to them, too.

Because supervisors and managers are the ones who must plan for the future of their organizations . . . the ones who have the headaches of "personnel problems," the problems of people who aren't doing their jobs . . . who quit . . . who became ill and are unable to do their jobs . . . and who, then, have *big problems*.

If you come along, and if you get to know those supervisors, you may turn out to be the solution to one of those problems.

If that is true, you'll be pleasantly surprised at how easy it is to get hired. In fact, you might find it difficult to "get away."

Ask For An Interview Even If There Are No Openings

Interviewing when there are no jobs is *not* a waste of time.

No jobs today? Maybe jobs tomorrow.

Ask for an interview. Afterward, thank the person in writing. Ask questions in the interview. Show you are interested. Read up on the company and the field before you go in, so you can ask intelligent questions about them, not stupid questions about health insurance, vacations, and fringe benefits.

Stay in touch afterward. Let them know you're interested.

How about the "sneak-in" interview, the one advocated by people who say you should try to get in for an interview by asking for "advice" or by asking someone to "evaluate my resume" when you are *really* looking for *a job*!

Sorry, folks. Honesty really does pay.

Don't lie to get in to see someone. They're smarter than you think, and you are likely to get "permanently UNhired" by that organization when the person discovers you've "sneaked in."

This isn't networking.

Networking is something which works for everyone, not just for you.

Keep Following Up

Stay in touch with people in your network.

Send thank you notes.

Send cartoons. Or articles from the professional journals.

Don't be a pest. Don't be "too aggressive." Once every once-in-a-while is enough. That means once every month or so.

Find ways to stay in touch. Be creative.

Send Resumes

Just because you've sent one resume doesn't mean they still have it.

Just because they sent it to someone else, doesn't mean that person has it.

They've probably lost it.

Remind them. Send another.

Attach a note:

> *"Thanks again for considering my resume. In case you need another, here's an extra copy."*

Call!

Call again. Call to see if they need more information. Call to see if there's anything else you should be doing. Call to see if they would like you to contact references. Or to get transcripts or credentials.

Call to see when you should call the next time.

If you detect a tone of annoyance in the voice of a secretary or a manager or a supervisor, say that you don't want to call too frequently, but that you are usually away from a phone and wanted to be certain you made yourself available, that you showed through an occasional phone call just how interested you really are in the opportunity with their organization.

Send Notes

Remember, send *good* notes. Short notes. Classy notes. And flawless notes, without smudges, dirt.

Notes and stationery should be "in good taste." If you somehow skipped over the chapter about "Packaging and Delivering a Resume" (Chapter 5), go back and read it.

And always, in writing, in person, in social gatherings, be *seen and heard* "in good taste."

One 44 year-old university business administration graduate, retired from the armed services, and recently re-trained in his newly-chosen field of computer science, decided to be seen everywhere . . . to "network his way to a job" after other methods had failed him.

This is usually a good idea.

Be he executed it poorly.

He wore a cheap polyester suit and a wide polyester tie, years after wide ties were passe. (Polyester ties are *always* passe!)

He wore long sideburns, which is fine for a costume party, bad for business.

Two years later, after hundreds of applications and interviews, and after networking his way through every organization in his city, he's still without a job in his field of computer science.

He looks like a "2" when he could look like a "10." He talks when he should listen. And he brags about his service experiences, instead of asking "I'm interested in you" questions of the people he meets.

He's a loser. But even worse: he doesn't know it.

Use The *Yellow Pages*

If you run out of ideas, use the *Yellow Pages* as a source of ideas.

You'll see how many thousands of places there are, how many thousands of jobs exist, and you'll get ideas about networking, people to contact, and even places to visit.

Should you write to places you see listed in the *Yellow Pages*?

Not if you can *network* your way to meet people who work there.

Always go through someone you know, to get to see or meet or visit with someone, or some place, you do not know.

Don't "go in cold," without an introduction, unless you've failed miserably to network your way into a contact.

Going in cold usually results in failure, especially if you're looking for favors, time, interviews, or if you should wander in at a particularly busy time.

Walk In, Anyway

Want to try it now? Just going in cold?

Try this, if you must:

- Prepare. Read about the company, the field. Or go in, ask for information about the organization, then leave until you've had a chance to read it.

- Look good. Dress up, not down. Remember that dressing up is a way of paying respect to the people you're visiting, or people you are with.

- Tell the receptionist, truthfully, that this kind of firm interests you, that you have been reading about it, and that you're considering entering a company like this as a career, as the next step.

- Ask if there is anyone in the firm you might talk to. See if anyone might have 10 minutes to spare for you, so that you could learn a bit more than you've read about.

- If the receptionist is friendly and helpful, thank him or her for the assistance. Get the receptionist's name, then thank the person in writing as soon as you get home.

- The same goes for the person you talk to about the company. Thank her or him, in writing, as soon as you return home.

- In your 10-minute chat, ask questions about what you've learned in your reading.

- Ask how they hire new employees. Ask if interviews are held regularly. Ask how you might obtain an interview to be considered for any new positions that might be opening up.

- Ask how you might learn more. Are there publications you might read? Is there a company newsletter, national, regional or local? Might you have a copy of his or her business card?

- Thank! In person . . . and in writing.

Some Tips For Negotiating Salary

Information about salary is sometimes difficult to come by.

If you go into an interview with *no* salary information, you deal from a position of weakness.

You should go into any interview with salary information about at least three things:

- Salary information about the field you're interested in,

- Salary information about the particular organization you're interviewing with,

- And salary information about other organizations in the same business as the organization you're interviewing with.

ASIDE: People, and out-of-work job applicants in particular, usually assume that they are Out of Control in the matter of salaries. This is not necessarily true.

If people are employed, and paid, to Solve Problems, the question becomes "What Is It Worth To The Employer To Solve This Problem?" rather than "What Will They Pay Me?"

No matter what skills you will be using on this job/any job/. . . someone else, in some other organization or in some other situation, will use those identical skills to solve the same or a very similar problem, and that person will be paid very, very well!

Your "Thinking" puts you "In Control" or "Out of Control" in the matter of salaries (and everything else!)

If you are thinking only within a small universe of Thinking and Possibility, the salary you will be able to command will be Small, and there will be No Possibility for it to be Large.

To increase your "Possibility of a Large Salary and Huge Earnings," you must enlarge your Thinking.

You must continue to increase your skills, your knowledge, and your worth.

When you begin to think that "I know enough now and don't need to know any more," you have put a cap on Your Thinking . . . and on Your Potential Earnings.

This small section, these words above, are well worth the price of this entire book. They are, in fact, priceless.

But only if you use them.

Salaries And Earnings In Your Chosen Field

How do people in your field earn their living?

Are they salaried? Are they paid on the basis of their output, their production? Do they receive bonuses? For what? Are their salaries reviewed? How often?

There are *many* more questions to ask than these.

Create some of your own.

Write down the things you would like to know about salaries, earnings, bonuses and potential earnings in your chosen field.

_____

_____

_____

_____

_____

_____

You should go into any interview with knowledge of the going rate for the industry, for specific jobs within that industry, knowledge of the growth factors and the non-growth factors.

You can obtain this information from the library. Or from your state or provincial employment service.

Know the ranges, from start-at-the-bottom to at-the-very-top.

If you go into an interview without this information you will be Out Of Control.

Psychologists would say you are "at effect," rather than "at cause."

Know what salary information you want. Then find it.

How Does This Organization Pay Its People?

Companies and organizations do not willingly give out salary information.

In fact, some organizations have been known to fire employees who violate a signed agreement that states:

> *"I will not discuss my earnings with my fellow workers inside this organization or with people outside this organization."*

How, then do you find out? From friends, relatives, neighbors, or colleagues.

Don't crassly ask, "How much money do people like you make?"

But do ask light, tactful questions such as "How much do you think someone in this position might make at ABC Distributors? Is there any way to find out what they pay, and what the earnings potential is at ABC?"

Any organization's pay scale is part of its reputation.

And if you ask around, ask enough people, and if you ask tactfully, you *can* find out the answers.

If you go into an interview without knowing, you haven't done enough homework/research, and you will not be in Full Control.

Salary Information In Other Organizations

The more you know about what other organizations are paying their people, the more Control you will have in the interview with Your Chosen Organization . . . or, at least, in the interview with Whatever Company you're lucky enough to have an interview with.

This, too, you can discover through the public or university libraries in your city, through books written about salaries in various fields, or from the local office of your state or provincial job/employment/unemployment office.

How To Answer "The Big Question"

After a pleasant, possibly successful interview, The Big Question usually comes up.

You *hope* it comes up.

If it does, you can usually conclude that "they're interested in me."

The Big Question, of course, is:

> ***"How much money are you looking for?"***

If they ask you this, they're usually interested.

It's possible they're not interested, and that they are merely collecting information, so that they will be able to offer their #1 candidate an appropriate salary, but *usually*, it means "We're interested."

How do you answer the tough question, "How much will you take?"

If you've not done your homework/research, if you do not know the salary information about The Job, The Company and The Field, the likelihood is that you will not do very well in your reply.

Do the research, so that you can be In Control.

If you know the information, you can answer the question this way: you can provide information, not merely a reply.

Employers always like information. They appreciate it, and if you can enlighten them about an important subject, you, too, will be appreciated.

You do *not* want to answer the question directly. You do not want, then, to "name an amount of money."

Everything "depends." In life, everything "depends."

Life is full of trade-offs.

So, too, is your job and the job offer you are negotiating for.

It might be the best job in the world, but for $8,000 annually, it wouldn't be.

It might be fun, but if you're working with dolts, with narrow-minded people, it wouldn't be.

So provide information . . . information which will allow the other person in the room to "handle the situation about your salary situation."

Here is a *good* way to answer the "How much money are you looking for?" question:

- "The job is much more important to me than the money is."

- "This organization is exactly what I am looking for."

- "I've been doing some salary research, a personal project, on my own . . . just to be aware of what's going on in the field and to see what people with my kind of background are worth these days."

- "From what I've been able to find out, by researching and by talking to people in the field, it seems that *most* of the people with my kind of background and experience and talents and skills . . . that **most** of those people . . . are starting out, the people at my level, somewhere in the neighborhood of _____ to _____.

  ASIDE: The two numbers you should mention are those which constitute a range of salaries. Be truthful: mention the almost-lowest amount, and the highest amount you've discovered that people are earning in this job, solving these kinds of problems.

You can include, or not include, fringe benefits and bonuses in these amounts. Use your discretion in making the decision to include or not include these factors.

The interviewer's question to you was: "How much do you want?"

Have you answered it?

No.

But you have provided some *information*, some excellent *guidelines*, for him or her to conclude that (1) you are interested, (2) you are somewhat flexible and not rigid, (3) the negotiations can now begin, and (4) you have provided, by stating information, a framework for the negotiations. . . and made the other person's job easier.

You have also (by providing information which comes from your Research) assume a position of "In Control."

That, my friends, is almost *magic*!

How many people do *you* know, in an interview situation, who know how to be *in control* in the salary situation?

What Comes Next?

After you have provided this information, you *stop talking*.

Notice the interviewer's response, the expression, the timing of his or her next words. Read the interviewer's eyes, as well as listening to the next words this person says.

If those next words are "That's no problem," you may have positioned yourself as "Too Low," "Too Inexpensive," "Too Cheap."

Is it, now, too late? Are you "boxed in" to the range you have mentioned?

No. Of course not.

You can negotiate fringe benefits, flexible time, additional vacation, profit sharing, bonuses, and virtually anything else.

You can even negotiate a much higher salary.

All you have said thus far is that:

"Some people, in some organizations and in some situations, are earning money which generally ranges from X to Y, but that this amount may be considerably greater when everything else is figured in."

You have not stated that "I want _____," or that "I need _____ to live and to support my family."

Employers are not interested in your needs, your desire for a better home, your fulfilling a lifelong dream for a sports car, or in a list of your monthly expenses.

They are interested in solving their problems, in hiring the best possible person to do that, in hiring a person who "fits in," and in paying a reasonable amount of money to accomplish these things.

A word of warning: some employers are downright cheap. They were. They are. And they will continue to be. Watch out for them! They never change!

A young man I know works for one of them. He's always the #1 or #2 producer. His sales are excellent, and so is his knowledge of his field. In 1988, he earned $15,000.

He has a college degree in psychology, is attractive and intelligent, but he works for an employer who has been, is, and will be "cheap."

If you've done your homework correctly, you'll avoid wasting your time talking to people like this employer.

"New Age" employers realize that when their employees do well and are happy, employers and their organizations will do well and will provide happy places in which to work.

"Old Age" employers build an organization by which and through which *they* can profit, and "the employees be damned."

Simple research and enlightening conversations with friends and associates can help you discover the "Old Age" employers before you solicit their fruitless favors and worthless workplaces.

A Final Word On Money

The wiser you get, the more you realize that health and happiness are everything . . . and that money is nothing.

But at about the same time in your life, you will realize, or you may have already realized, that money is power. . . and that it often gives you the power to live a lifestyle which may create the possibility for you to have health and happiness.

You are not locked in.

You have the power of choice to do what you want, to do it where you want to do it, to do it by yourself, or to do it for an employer who, like you, recognizes the magnificence of life and in supporting and sustaining the good things which life is and which it can bring to anyone who makes these things a possibility for himself or herself.

Do not have an inflated idea of the value of the solutions which you can bring to the workplace.

But do have an honest recognition of the uniqueness of your potential.

Be willing to continue your journey toward that potential, within the universe of an employer, firm or organization which allows you the joys of the journey.

Epilogue

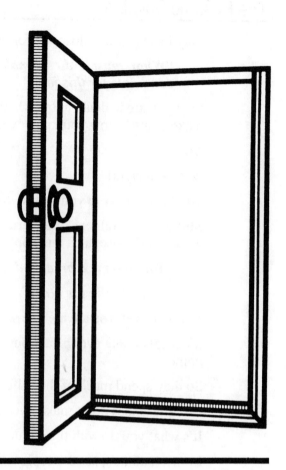

Is This The End?

Adopt "The Philosophy Of Job Hunting"

This is the final chapter.

But this isn't the end.

People who know, people far more knowledgeable than I am, tell us that life is more worthwhile, more satisfying, and more productive if it has a *purpose*.

A purpose means that you have a *vision* of where you hope to go in your life . . . what you hope to *be* and *become*.

In the 1970s, a certain brewery told us that "You only go around once in life, so grab for all the *gusto* you can!"

If they meant *alive-ness*, I think they were right on target.

Life is about being *alive* and about living your *purpose*.

Job hunting, too, should have a *purpose*.

A specific goal.

And it is best lived out if you adopt a Philosophy of Job Hunting, a kind of *purpose* for doing what you are going to do.

May I suggest a philosophy for your job-hunt?

> *"What must I do to make certain that I am the number one candidate for this job?"*

So if you are in doubt about whether to do that little extra something that would make you #1, now you know what to do.

Do it!

And do it right!

You have a *duty* to yourself to do your best!

Millions and millions of advertising dollars have been spent to impress people with two philosophies that apply more to life than they do to hamburgers.

> *"You deserve a break today."*

> *"You! You're the One!"*

And you are! You are the one who can give yourself the break you deserve.

Most folks take every little bump in the road as a signal to turn back and go home.

So they spend much of their life going back where they started.

Circumstances don't make lives good. Or bad.

It's what you do with the circumstances that makes a difference.

In my seminars, some people actually complain that we talk about *empowerment* and about "doing something *special* with your life," rather than just existing in it.

Peter Ueberroth, winner of Time Magazine's "Man of the Year" award and the man who turned the Olympics in Los Angeles into a phenomenal success, gives us a valuable lesson when he says:

> *"Authority is only 20 percent given, and it is 80 percent taken!"*

Don't wait for someone to give you something.

Take responsibility for taking it.

Take it honestly.

Earn it.

Do it with integrity.

Life isn't easy.

But it *is* always an adventure, if you choose to make it one.

Psychologist and positive-thinker Denis Waitley talks of the "poor TV watcher," sitting there, bored to tears and wasting a life, wasting so many talents.

While actors and actresses in a far-away studio have the time of their lives. Being well-paid.

And doing what they love most—acting.

Act!

Living is an *active* art !

The more you *do* in this life, the happier and more satisfied you will be.

The more you give to others, the happier *you* will be.

And the greater part of your life's activities you devote to the things you live to do *most* and do *best*, the more full and productive your life will become.

And you will contribute to the goodwill being done on the planet.

Existence is the booby prize.

Living is First Place!

If you don't *live*, you lose.

Be a winner.

Then you'll never worry about having to say, "I can't remember what I wanted to be when I grew up . . . but I know this isn't it."

Take charge of your life. Make it living

Alive

Make it work for you!